Foreword

Young Writers' Bust-A-Rhyme competition is a showcase for secondary school pupils to share their poetic creativity and inspiration. Selecting the poems has been challenging and immensely rewarding. The effort and imagination invested by these young writers makes their poems a pleasure to enjoy reading time and time again.

Young Writers was established in 1991 to nurture creativity in our children and young adults, to give them an interest in poetry and an outlet to express themselves. Seeing their work in print will encourage them to keep writing and become our poets of tomorrow.

Publishing Children's Poetry For 19 Years

Bust-A-Rhyme

Giving verse a voice

Staffordshire

Edited by Helen Davies

First published in Great Britain in 2010 by:

Young Writers
Remus House
Coltsfoot Drive
Peterborough
PE2 9JX
Telephone: 01733 890066
Website: www.youngwriters.co.uk

Book Design by Spencer Hart, Ali Smith & Tim Christian

SB ISBN 978-1-84924-799-3

Contents

The Poems

Think Teenagers, Think Bad?

Are all babies the same? I don't think so, do you?
And adults, are they all the same through and through?
Do all toddlers toddle at a certain same time?
And do all the elderly all whinge and whine?

No, I don't think so, that's just not true,
There's so much difference between me and you.
So please don't be in such a great rush,
To tar all teens with the same big brush.

I'm not yet a teen, I've a year to go,
But then won't you like me? I really don't know.
On reaching that age do they all get the blame,
For the odd one or two that give them a bad name?

Drunken yobs are seen on the telly,
But it's only a few, it's not that many,
Fighting, swearing, graffiti and drugs,
Is what's generally thought of 'those teenage thugs'.

But what's not reported is the good that they do,
They don't make the news so let's name just a few,
Charity work and sponsored runs,
Learning at school and passing exams,
Pushing the boundaries in science, sport, art,
You may not believe it but they can be smart.
Questioning politics, forming ideas,
Making decisions about their careers.

These are the people who once were you,
And these are the people who I'll be too,
And if I decide to wear a hoodie,
It won't make me bad, I'll still be a goody.

Megan Allingham (12)
Clayton Hall Business & Language College

My First Day Of High School

I woke up in the morning
And got out of my bed
I looked in the mirror
And saw a spot on my head
'Oh no, not today, I'm going to school
The other kids will see it
I'll feel such a fool!'
My mum saw it, she said
'It will be just fine.'
But what does she know?
So I started to whine
I walked to the shop
To meet with my mates
There were a couple of girls
We could get some dates
We carried on walking
We finally got there
'I'm sure nobody will notice
I've got ginger hair.'
Class bell rang and in I walked
The kid next to me did nothing but talk
The day was long
But I enjoyed it a lot
And what was the best?
No one noticed my spot!
We made our way home down Northwood Lane
And I was sure I wouldn't feel so bad
When tomorrow I did it again.

Matthew Smith (11)
Clayton Hall Business & Language College

Amongst Them

I stand amongst them,
A small shadow amongst a sea of cool,
Comments come my way, 'nerd', 'freak', 'Moaning Myrtle'
It hurts inside, but I carry on,
Trying to ignore, trying to forget,
The hurt that I feel inside.

I sit amongst them,
A small shadow amongst a sea of cool,
I do my work, I'm not a nerd,
I just want a future,
All 'cause I want to change my life,
'Cause so far it's been bad.

I'm here amongst them,
A small shadow amongst a sea of cool.
Hated, yet still here,
Wishing that the bullying would stop.
Wishing that I was like them,
Wishing that I was cool,
But I can't be, 'cause I'm unique, I'm me.

Liana Jane Bourne (13)
Clayton Hall Business & Language College

Perfect World?

Has this place ever been a perfect world
Where happiness and joy to everyone was heard?

Has this place ever been a perfect road,
A break from litter and gangs of boys and girls?

Has this place ever been a perfect shop
Where people feast off drugs and drink; more than one drop?

Has this place ever been a perfect house,
With the scream of an abused child's mind full of doubt?

So has this place ever been perfect you ask?

This question is your task . . .

Jemimah Lack (11)
Clayton Hall Business & Language College

Weather

When the dark
clouds cover up the
sky, I feel lonely.

When the sunshine
comes and brightens up
my day, I feel happy.

When the storm
comes and rains
I feel down and sad.

When the lightning
strikes the Earth
I feel angry.

When the
snowflakes touch
my tongue, I
feel lovely.

Phoebe Markham (11)
Clayton Hall Business & Language College

Terror For A Teenager

Argue, argue, argue, ripping down the house,
While I sit - grounded - as quiet as a mouse.

Not enough attention, never about me,
All the attention, evading my family.

Loads of homework in for the next day,
They don't listen, I never have my say.

I'm really sorry Sir, I didn't do that in science,
My parents argue, they haven't got an alliance.

I'm in detention for something that wasn't fair,
Teacher sitting at his desk - a dragon at his lair.

The arguing stopped, the pressure was gone,
Everyone smiling as my report shone.

Mark Bollington (12)
Clayton Hall Business & Language College

First Time Surfer

I'm sitting on my surfboard,
Singing a song,
I'm gazing at the horizon,
Wanting waves to come along,
The sun is shining strongly,
Beating down on the sand,
Seagulls swooping through the sky,
Children building sandcastles nearby,
The tide is finally turning,
Things are looking fine,
I can see the white horses coming,
My day is beginning to shine,
I run down to the water,
Waves now crashing over my feet,
I jump onto my board and swim out to sea,
I'm standing up for the first time
It's victory for me.

Emma Dodd (11)
Clayton Hall Business & Language College

A New Beginning!

'Twas the night before my very first day at Clayton High School . . .
A very sleepless night to say the least.
My mind was in turmoil with worry.
So scared was I of the beast!

I entered the grounds before me,
My heart skipping every beat,
But in the back of my mind were my mum's words,
'Don't worry, you'll be fine!'

My eyes flitted all around me as I felt like a teeny weeny ant.
These people scurrying by me were as big as a giant.

The end of my day was upon me,
I walked out smiling with glee,
As I'd made so many new friends,
I felt like a brand new me!

Olivia Richardson (11)
Clayton Hall Business & Language College

I Love You!

Mum, when they said you were going to die,
I didn't want to say goodbye.
I refused that it could be true
With what happened to my dad I didn't want it to happen to you.
I was so tired of waiting for good news,
I kind of gave up hope.
It's been over a year now Mum
Since the angels took you away.
I still miss you every single day.
You were more than my mother,
You were my best friend too,
You always used to listen to me
And I want you to know I love you!
Mum I can never say goodbye to you
Because I could never bear the pain.
Instead I say I love you Mum, until we meet again.

Rebecca Swift (13)
Clayton Hall Business & Language College

New School Bully!

She stands there tall, glaring at us all
Making us all feel so small
She takes our dinner and our money for the bus
And she tells us all not to fuss
We hate this school
It's just not cool
So I'm telling her to stop
This has pushed me to the top
So I walk straight past
Trying to go fast
She tries to stop me but not this time
I say, 'No! Pick on someone else this time!'
And now I love this school
It's just so cool
No more bullies
Just my friends.

Molly Ryles (13)
Clayton Hall Business & Language College

Why Me?

She has to target me out of everyone in the school.
Is it the way I look, is it the way I dress?
Does she think that I'm uncool?
She follows me round like an infection or a tumour.
For the one opportunity to laugh at me or spread a rumour.
'Tell anyone, you're dead!' she says,
A wicked grin across her face.
With my hands, sweating, body itching,
Heart beating at a fast pace.
I have to tell someone, if it's tomorrow or today,
It's the only way to make the bullying go away
And now I'm glad I told someone
And I know I'm not alone.
It doesn't matter how you tell someone,
If it's face to face or on the phone.

Jess Bates (12)
Clayton Hall Business & Language College

Just Give Me A Chance

Some people think I'm bad
Others think that I'm mad
Some people think that I want to be seen
Others think that I'm a crazy teen.
Some people think that I'm a crook
Others think about how I look
But I'm not a crook or bad or mad
In fact those words make me really sad
I've got a smile
That could go a mile
Just let me explain
That I'm not a pain
And that I'm really quite good
If you please would
Just give me a chance.

Harriet Arthur (12)
Clayton Hall Business & Language College

Untitled

Feelings are somethin' you can't deny
They're in your head all the time
Stressed
Depressed
Happy or
Sad
Feeling good
Feeling bad
When someone dies your feelings are hurt bad
The birth of a child makes a father's heart glad
I look through my window
And wonder why
At the different feelings I have inside
The freedom I feel when I ride my bike
A racing heart, the feeling I like.

Elliott Barrow (14)
Clayton Hall Business & Language College

I Will Always Be Rising

(Inspired by 'Still I Rise' by Maya Angelou)

You may write me down in history,
With your bitter feelings about me,
You may dislike me in a good way,
But still, like happiness, I will always rise.

Does my appearance upset you?
Do you think I belong here?
If it does and if I don't belong here,
It doesn't bother me,
I will still be rising like dust.

Just like the moon and the sun,
Just like day and night,
Just like my age,
I will always be rising.

Thomas Smith (11)
Clayton Hall Business & Language College

My Dream

My dream is to become a singer or a footballer
My dream is to become rich
My dream is to become really famous
My dream is to become really cool
My dream is to get all the ladies
My dream is to get a really nice house
My dream is to get a really nice car
My dream is to sell loads of albums
My dream is to play for a top club
My dream is to play with brilliant players
My dream is to have an iPhone
My dream is to have an iPod Touch
My dream is to have a plasma screen TV
And they're my dreams!

Sam Dean (11)
Clayton Hall Business & Language College

My School

I go to a school called Clayton High
We always, always, always try.
Some teachers are nice, some teachers are mean,
Some teachers are funny and always keen.
For English there's Miss Gimbert in room 44,
For maths there's Mr Findlay in room 30,
For creative there's Mr Gallagher and maybe Miss Mitchell,
For French, Mr Green and German Mr Prime.
(Who sets out homework all the time!)
And last but not least for my form tutor Mrs Milns,
Who is extremely nice!
And that's my time at Clayton High,
I hope you get a place there, see ya! Bye!

Saira Irfan (11)
Clayton Hall Business & Language College

Live Your Life

L ove everyone in your life, and don't have enemies
I nvite new people into your life and make new friends
V isit new places and experience new things
E veryone deserves a second chance.

Y ou are what you are, don't change for anyone
O pen up to people, don't keep anything bottled up
U ndo any bad past memories and look forward to the future
R espect everyone around you.

L isten to advice and take everything on board
I dolise your elders and learn things from them
F ollow your dreams, you can do whatever you want to do
E njoy the experience of trying new things.

Laura Thompson (13)
Clayton Hall Business & Language College

Christmas Eve

A man and his son
Were walking through the woods,
The trees were all white,
The ground was all white
And the ponds were all frozen.

They could see smoke coming
Out of the chimneys of houses,
His son asked, 'Why is everything so white?'
His dad replied, 'It's Christmas Eve tonight.'

The boy could hear the birds playing a tune,
While he was saying to himself,
'It's Christmas Eve soon.'

Thomas Brown (11)
Clayton Hall Business & Language College

A Beautiful Day

The sun is shining,
The music beats,
The birds are singing,
People meet.

Fun and laughter,
Dance and song,
The people are happily,
Going along.

Animals running,
The children play,
Today it is a beautiful
Day!

Rachel Hulson
Clayton Hall Business & Language College

Why? - Why Do You Ignore Me?

Why don't you talk to me?
Why do you stand there and watch my heartbreak?
After everything I have done I don't even get a, 'Hi!'
All I get is a look, a stare, not a smile.
You don't understand how upset I am,
So why act like nothing happened?
Every time I am near you, you look, I look back
Then that's it,
If I smile or say, 'Hi,' you look away.
What have I done?
Why are you doing this to me?
I gotta know, I need to do something!

Bethanie Spiers (13)
Clayton Hall Business & Language College

The Wolf

The wolf howls on a cliff's edge,
Under the black, starry night,
Being menacing he sits dangerously,
His sleek silver coat glistens in the moonlight,
When he opens his mouth,
You can see his sharp fangs,
He sniffs for his prey,
A gunshot in the distance bangs,
He sees a deer by a large rock,
He swiftly runs after it on all fours,
The deer falls to the ground,
He rips it with his huge jaws.

Matt Stride (14)
Clayton Hall Business & Language College

Oh Dear!

It was a dark, stormy night,
Nothing was stirring, not even a mite.
Nothing to hear and nothing to fear.
But there was one thing that wanted to sing
Which was Judy's pet dog, Moody.
He barked the whole night away,
Until there was nothing else to say.
He woke me up in the morning,
Just as the day was dawning.
As I was about to dress,
He made a big mess!
'Oh no Moody! Mum will be so broody!'

Harry Robinson (13)
Clayton Hall Business & Language College

The Streets

If you were an old lady struggling on your feet
Would you like to be passing the youth on the streets?
With the graffiti and the crime, drugs and jail time.
Would you feel safe seeing smiles on faces
As they're vandalising public places?
In their trainers and hoodies
Underage mums pushing their buggies
With a fag in their right hand and a beer in their left
Fighting with knives until someone is dead
If you were an old lady struggling on your feet
Would you like to be passing the youth on the streets?

Jordan Hughes (11)
Clayton Hall Business & Language College

Thoughts In My Head

I sleep with one eye open so I can't dream
About the time I was left in pieces like broken glass.
My heart is still on standby.
They all say the feelings will pass.

I let the tears roll down my cheeks, I'm alive yet so dead.
I'll try to make the memories fade, thoughts in my head.

Here we are, back to the start.
This is my life today, no colour, all black and grey.
Kick start my heart.
Help the memories fade.

Demi-Elle Khetia (13)
Clayton Hall Business & Language College

Love Hurts

Love is like a dagger digging in my side.
Searching for the one right.
He seems to hide, from my view,
So someone please help me find my true,
From the endless deep dark.
Thank you for helping me find the only one,
The one for me,
The boy who brings the light to my life
From the dark, lonely hole.
Thank you.

Rosa Dilling (13)
Clayton Hall Business & Language College

My Bird, Ozzy

Ozzy is a cockatiel,
Can you imagine how he makes me feel . . .?
When I leave the room he starts to squeal,
When I let him out of his cage he causes a rampage,
He won't let me do my homework, he pecks my pen!
I think he needs a hen!
He is not like a dove,
But he gives me lots of love.
I love my Ozzy.

Jemima Fowler (11)
Clayton Hall Business & Language College

Feelings

Happiness is great, it makes you want to jump
Sadness is awful, a waterfall of tears
Anger is revenge, on the ones who are bad
Fear is cold, ghosts flying around you
There are many feelings in you
But these are just a few.

Leah Bentley (13)
Clayton Hall Business & Language College

There's This Guy At School

There's this guy at school, he beats people up,
But no one grasses 'cause he'll pick on them.
This same guy at school, he calls you names,
But teachers never hear him.
This guy at school, he doesn't do his homework,
So he nicks mine instead.
This guy at school, he copies my work and is now in every top set.
This guy at school has no GCSEs now,
Because he didn't listen to what the teacher said.

James Attwood (13)
Clayton Hall Business & Language College

My Father!

I had to do as I was told
When he went up to town,
I was left on my own,
With tears, sadness in my eyes!

Mum got very mad
When she got back,
Because she knew I was on my own
He was spotted on his own in town!

Louis Lear (11)
Clayton Hall Business & Language College

Summer's Night

It's late at night in the summer, where all the cities are dead,
The relaxing noise of silence, people sweaty in their beds.
The soft rustling of the trees, made by the gentle summer breeze,
People awake at night, because the density is so tight.
Tourists sleeping, dreaming of the next summer's day.
But when they wake up in the morning, those dreams are shed away.
At the end of all the summer through all the sweat and thirst
Is the beginning of autumn and the sleepless winter's nights.

Chris Bagnall (13)
Clayton Hall Business & Language College

I Have . . .

I have hatred, burning away my love
I have conflict, taking away my care
I have anger, forcing away my family
I have loneliness, dragging my soul away
I have despair, stealing my life
I have . . . nothing, just an empty void.

David Fox-Wells (13)
Clayton Hall Business & Language College

All Is Well After Death

Death is nothing at all,
I have only slipped away into the next room.
Laugh as we always laughed
At the little jokes we enjoyed together,
Play, smile, think of me, pray for me.

Ishan Lakhani (13)
Clayton Hall Business & Language College

The Terrible Football Match

The only memory I have,
Is of a terrible football match.

We were losing eight - nil,
I just couldn't chill.

There were bodies everywhere,
It made me pull out my hair.

I was shouting like mad,
The rumours were really bad.

The fans got caught calling,
So very verbally in the sunny morning.

After the terrible football match,
I thought there must be a catch.

Sam Rowley (12)
Edensor Technology College

Armada Poem

The Armada was coming, we would all cry,
The Armada was coming as we flowed by.
All the ships,
Crashed into bits.
The Spanish were ready for pain and loss,
While Sir Francis Drake was awarded boss!
If the English fought with all their might,
They would win the fight.
The Armada was coming, we would all cry,
The Armada was coming, we would all die.
The fire was as hot as the sun,
As we said goodbye to our son.
The rumour of Sir Francis put him to shame,
The Spanish thought the English were lame.
It didn't last,
It was not fast.
Suddenly it happened . . . *Bang!*
There was a big explosion.
The battle had already begun.
The Armada was coming, we nearly all died,
The Armada was coming, out went the cry.
There were splinters of wood,
Bodies scattered,
Blood sinking into the sea.
It all happened at once,
The English never gave up.
The Spanish grew tired,
The English had won!
The Armada was coming, the English won,
The Armada was done.
The Spanish had to travel all around Spain,
While the English were in no pain.

Demi-Rose Cotterill (11)
Edensor Technology College

Liverpool Game

Kick, kick, kick,
Liverpool score a goal,
Jumping up and down,
Just scored the goal,
Steven Gerrard gets the ball,
Passes it to number 9,
The wild crowd go wild,
'Hooray, hooray!'
See the ball,
Someone scores,
'What's happened?'
'You just missed the goal!'

Half-time,
Oh no,
But it's fun to see the score,
That team,
What a team,
My team,
Which team?
Just a team,
Let's see if we can win the cup,
Maybe not . . .

Half-time over,
Hooray, hooray,
The crowd goes wild now,
Fernando Torres is number 9,
Steven Gerrard is number 8,
Score, score,
Yeah, yeah,
Jump up and down,
For a goal.

Nastassja Sarah Porter (11)
Edensor Technology College

My Time Has Come

The final day has come at last,
Time to leave behind my past,
Time to leave behind my friends,
Time to start all over again,
They look and I smile like the sun,
But inside I don't feel so fun,
7 weeks and I'll be gone,
My last year in school is done.

I cry and cry and cry some more,
I cry so much my eyes go sore,
It isn't just me there is more
People whose eyes are all sore,
It is over when Mum gives me a call,
And there isn't a dry eye in the hall,
'I'm going to miss this place,' I said,
As I tuck myself into bed.

The summer holidays go so fast,
That the dreaded day is here at last,
I go into the mighty hall,
Turns out it isn't so bad at all,
All the teachers are really nice,
They show us around and give us advice,
The first day at high school is lots of fun,
Too bad soon it'll be gone.

Gregory Street (11)
Edensor Technology College

Edensor

E xcited
D evastated
E xcited for a new school
N ew school and new world
S hy
O verexcited
R emember to wake up at 6.30am.

Zoe Marie Mayer (11)
Edensor Technology College

New Moon

I can still feel you near,
Though you're far away, I fear
Of all the things I left unsaid.
Did you mean to have left me dead?
What is my life without you?
What is the night with no moon?
I may turn my cheek
From this deep miscellany of pain,
But I will always be haunted,
By your memory in vain.
Now as I watch you fly away,
A descant soul into the horizon,
I beg for you to be forever free.
I wish I could run fast,
But there's no running from this past.
In time, I may attempt to forget,
But you I will never regret.
Slowly, yet surely, time seems to pass,
Though I can never outlast,
Our love,
My tears,
Standing below this new moon,
I vow to always love you.

Hayley Farrington (12)
Edensor Technology College

Roses

Roses in the day, they look so bright
But if one died I would just cry.
I have a rose in my hair.
I take it everywhere.
If it falls, I fall too,
In the night I put it to bed.
Also I dream of it in my head.
If it's not there I can't bear the pain inside.
Some days and nights I wonder what's happened to my rose.

Keenan Bettany (11)
Edensor Technology College

The Times We Spent Together

Your name is often spoken,
My thoughts are with you still,
You have not been forgotten,
What's more you never will.
If Heaven had a phone,
I would call you everyday,
To tell you that I miss you,
More than words could say.

There are no words to say how I feel,
No length of time will help me heal.
I miss you more each passing year,
My lifelong wish to have you here.

I sat beside your bed not knowing what to do.
I held your hand and touched your face
And gently talked to you
I told you that I loved you
And wanted you to stay
But in my heart
I had realised you had to slip away.

Aleena Mohammed (11)
Edensor Technology College

Sadness

I'm feeling really sad today
My best friend's left, he's gone away
We thought that we'd hang out for life
And even when we got a wife
We'd live next door and help with kids
Make sure we'd close the dustbin lids
Oh well, I hope he does alright
Cos all we really did was fight
Today I'm off out up the park
To check if anyone wants a lark
Then maybe I won't feel so sad
I prefer it when I'm happy and glad.

Nabeel Iqabal (12)
Edensor Technology College

Fashion

After school I always go
Into the shop to see what's on show . . .
There are stripy socks and sparkly trousers,
And even the most ridiculous blouses!

After school I always go
Into the shop to see what's on show . . .
There are baggy trousers and denim jeans,
With bulging pockets and fluorescent yellow seams!

After school I always go
Into the shop to see what's on show . . .
There are knee-high boots and mini skirts,
Red spotty pants and awesome checked shirts!

After school I always go
Into the shop to see what's on show . . .
There are pretty long dresses that are in the sale,
Hats and scarves for the wind and hail!

After school I always go
Into the shop to see what's on show . . .

Caitlin Gifford (11)
Edensor Technology College

Feelings

We all have feelings me and you,
Sometimes we're happy, sometimes we're blue.
When something scares you, you might feel afraid,
We all feel proud of something we've made
When some of us want to know more
We feel a bit curious,
When we slip on the floor, we kind of feel furious
We sometimes feel lonely, when we don't have anything to do.
We sometimes feel a bit of hunger
When there's nothing to chew.
We all feel excited, when we make a new friend.
I'm feeling sad because my poem has to end.

Aisha Zafar (12)
Edensor Technology College

The Key Of Love

Your love is like a key
and my heart is like a diary.
I have so many secrets,
what I thought I'd never share,
then everything changed when you came along.
I let out all my hopes, dreams and wishes.

Our love is like a lasting flower forever in bloom,
growing as the days go by.
It grows stronger and more beautiful every day.
You have opened up my heart,
with your magic key of love,
and revealed love, hope and trust.

My heart had a magic door that opened,
and I'll love you for evermore.
You have made me realise that,
you're my long-lost love.
These are the reasons why you're
my true love. My only love.

Emily Morrey (11)
Edensor Technology College

Animal Cruelty

Once again I'm all alone
Waiting for some food.
I try and try to let out a cry
But my voice won't let me.

When my owner disappears
The bruises reappear.

I crawl up in a ball
Starving all night long.
Why does this have to happen
To any pet at all?

When my owner disappears
The bruises reappear.

Lauren Hulme (12)
Edensor Technology College

My Grandad

My grandad is a joy to watch
He talks a load of tosh
He is very funny
His personality is very sunny

My grandad is a clown
He makes me very proud
My grandad makes me laugh
He acts very daft

My grandad is my best friend
He drives me round the bend
My grandad is like Rip Van Winkle
He tends to fall asleep a lot

He is always looking at the clock
Having said a lot
I still love him a lot

My grandad.

Kirsty Bagguley (11)
Edensor Technology College

My Holiday Disaster

I was on holiday, backchatting my nan,
Feeling really keen,
Next thing I knew, I fell off the bowling green!
I badly gashed my knee,
My nan thought it was funny,
When she saw how bad it was she said,
'Come here, Honey.'
The first aiders came running,
To see if I was alright,
They got out a plaster and they put it on tight.
I was looking at my knee,
My nan thought I was messing,
She said, 'Serves you right,
That will teach you a lesson!'

Cloe Theraza Jade Smallwood (13)
Edensor Technology College

Love Is True

Valentine's Day is near,
Just wishing you were here.
So many years of loving you,
So many things that we've been through.

Still I can't find the reason,
Tell me why am I so much
In love with you?

Love is always a true dream,
So go and grab some heart ice cream.
Love is a happy feeling,
So let it be healing.

I love you more than a red rose.
So I will do you a pose.
Treasure this special day as it's only once a year.
I am sending you this poem with a sealed kiss,
Wishing you a happy Valentine's Day.

Lauren Chatwin (12)
Edensor Technology College

Feelings

At times I feel so happy, at times I feel so sad.
At times I get so angry, at times I get so mad.
My feelings annoy me when I get to school,
There are a group of kids who think I'm so uncool.
They always bully me and follow me
But other people do not see.
I try not to be angry, I try not to be unkind
But I can't stop calling them names and calling them blind.
I always try hard in lessons.
I always try not to listen to them and give them bad looks.
Then I get angry (because they are calling me names)
Then I throw lots of books.
I try to ignore them calling me names
And then I get so sad, I start being bad.

Chantelle Hankey (12)
Edensor Technology College

My First Day At Edensor

I woke up bright and early,
Headed for school feeling worried,
I spoke to my sister, she said,
'It's great, you'll have fun.'

My first day at Edensor,
I was nervous and scared,
I started to worry,
But nobody cared.

They said, 'Just try your best,
It's just like primary.
There's no need to be scared,
Just keep thinking of good things.

Toughen up, be strong,
You'll have a great day.'
I went in school, feeling nervous and worried,
So I kept saying to myself, 'You can do it!'

Danielle Dryden Coysh (11)
Edensor Technology College

Happiness

My face beams like the sun
When I'm happy
Smiling joyfully
But then it fades when the sun goes in
My happiness goes in the bin
But I will win it back
I slither like a snake trying to retrieve it
And then the dark sky disappears.
So the sun pops out
I get that fabulous feeling again
Where I get a tingle inside
I leave the sadness behind
And go back to smiling
My face beams like the sun.

Emily Birks (11)
Edensor Technology College

Feelings

Life, life is here
Life is there
You can eat an apple
Cut a pear
Life, life is loving
Loving, great
But loving, loving can be hate.

Hate, hate is also anger
Talking about you
Dissing you, not missing you
Thinking of words we cannot say
Locked up in an angry place.

Life is full of feelings
Feelings aimed at you
Life is full of feelings
Feeling always true.

Jessica Jade Smith (11)
Edensor Technology College

The Fight

Stay in there, in the light,
Stay here, where you must fight,
Win the battle with all your might,
To avoid the darkness of night.

It doesn't matter about our height,
Nor if the enemy is black or white,
Win the battle with all your might,
To avoid the darkness of night

Doesn't matter if you're right,
Nor if the enemy barks or bites,
Win the battle with all your might,
To avoid the darkness of the night,
The night full of darkness . . . of Hell.

James Oliver Dibden (11)
Edensor Technology College

My Dog

My dog was the cutest little thing,
Oh how he used to jump and do his thing,
Now he's gone, I feel so sad
But my heart whimpers his name.
Izzy, Izzy, that's the name,
My dog was the funniest little thing,
He was always barking my name,
In the morning when I was asleep,
He barked and barked and lay at my feet,
Now he's gone I feel so sad
But my heart whimpers his name,
Izzy, Izzy, that's the name,
Oh don't worry he's not dead,
He's just gone but he's stuck in my head,
Izzy, Izzy, I wish you were here,
Izzy, Izzy, my little dear.

Shanita Taylor (11)
Edensor Technology College

Inside The Fence

Ring, the vibration in my ears,
Why are they all so big,
Other children and my peers?
And the gates,
Are they to keep out the monsters, wolves and bad hates?
It's an island and we are all trapped,
Children longing to hear the muffled voices of children in hallways,
Meaning home time,
Rushing through crowded hallways,
A small child in a sea of tall, lank children always.
Maths is tough and the numbers they're plenty,
English paragraphs, how many?
Then there's PE, you might get to play ball.
Pay attention, do you want a detention?
Ring, the vibrating in my ears.
Finally after all.

Tiffany Woodward (12)
Edensor Technology College

Scary Place

I am haunted,
This is terrible,
When there is a shadow by my bed,
I curl up in my covers,
Because I am terrified.

I walk on my own with a shiver in my spine,
I can't sleep at night,
With the trees hitting my bedroom window,
I am alone in this scary place,
There will never be a smile upon my face.

I twist and turn in my bed,
Trying to think of better things,
I don't get sleep with a fright on my mind,
I am so scared,
Help me sleep at night.

Molly Lockett (11)
Edensor Technology College

Love Like This

In my life I'll never find,
A boy like you, so sweet and kind.
A boy who loves me like you do,
Someone who cares; someone who's you.
Our love is special
But jealousy is bad.
We make each other very sad.
But much of the time it is so good,
In my flower, you are my bud.
When we go our separate ways,
We'll say goodbye to all the days
When we loved and laughed and cried,
On that day my tears will not hide.

Lucy Ridgway (12)
Edensor Technology College

The Thought Swan

I glare upon the white feature,
Gliding across the lake.
As the creature slowly drifts away,
It becomes a grey blur.

Through the pupils of my eyes,
It becomes more clear.
I finally realise what I have seen,
As once again it draws near.

The long neck of a swan,
Reaches to see the blue sky.
As I look further I glare,
To see the baby ducks.

Kelly Louise Banner (12)
Edensor Technology College

Hallowe'en

Hallowe'en can be very scary
Some beasts and werewolves are really hairy
Little girls who are dressed as fairies or witches
Young boys running around screaming and shouting.

They knock on doors to trick or treat
All the while hoping for sweets
There are Hallowe'en costumes in all weird disguises
Goody bags packed full with candy prizes.

Hallowe'en parties all in full swing
Scary songs the children do sing
About goblins, vampires and witches and ghouls
Something to talk about tomorrow at school.

Joseph Heath (12)
Edensor Technology College

Beach Poem

Rubber rings on the beach,
People swimming in the sea,
It's really hot, it's really hot,
The waves go *smash, crash!*

People relaxing in the sun,
People burning their bums,
While other people are burning their tums.
Children playing with big rubber balls,
Children laughing like hyenas,
Adults chilling on a dinghy,
Sandwiches soggy from the blazing hot sun.

Paige Frost (11)
Edensor Technology College

Cats

Cats sleep anywhere
Any table
Any chair
Top of the piano
Window ledge
In a corner
On an edge
In an empty shoe box
Under the table
In the cupboard with your frocks
'Cause cats sleep anywhere!

Samira Sanam (11)
Edensor Technology College

Go To The Beach

See the waves going back and forth,
See people playing catch the ball.
Sitting down on my chair,
While the wind blows through my hair.

Chloe Louise Wiggins (11)
Edensor Technology College

The Match

As he sat watching his favourite team,
Suddenly his ears began to steam,
When the other team scored,
He punched the floor,
And let out a piercing scream.

It was the start of the second half,
The player scored off his calf,
Then the team scored again,
From an amazing pen,
My dad jumped up and waved his scarf.

Liam Harvey
Edensor Technology College

The Best Of Friends

The best of friends
Can change a frown into a smile
When you feel down.

The best of friends will understand
Your little trials and lend a hand.

The best of friends will always share
Because they care.

The best of friends are worth more than gold,
Give all the love a heart can hold.

Chloe Louise Coleman (11)
Edensor Technology College

Nightmare

Nightmares are horrible, they wake you through the night
Dreams are much nicer, they don't give you such a fright
Sometimes you can be chased or fall off a cliff
Most of the time when you wake up you end up being stiff
I know they can't be true but they seem so real
Most people say, 'Oh they're no big deal.'
But some nightmares, you can have them twice
And those ones aren't that nice
Nightmares are horrible, they wake you through the night
Dreams are much nicer, they don't give you such a fright.

Eleanor Astley (11)
Edensor Technology College

Untitled

I feel lonely,
I feel lost,
But worst of all I'm in the cold, cold frost.
All alone in the dark whilst I'm sleeping on
The bench in the park
Looking for money
Searching for clothes
But all I can find
Is a big bag
Of *bones!*

Joshua Jake Brammer (11)
Edensor Technology College

Love!

I can't explain my love for you.
I'm floating on clouds, when I'm by you.
Whenever you smile I go all blue.

You make my heart,
Feel like a never-ending sunset.
The red sky at night,
Shepherd's delight.
It's just like you, so warm and true,
But most of all I just love you!

Dana Payne (11)
Edensor Technology College

Still Haunting Me!

I know he's still haunting me,
How can this be?
I know my grandad is watching me,
When I lie in my bed,
Feel something cold touch my head,
I feel things rising from the dead,
Dare I open the window,
As he might go,
He's still haunting me, I just know.

Danni Royals (11)
Edensor Technology College

Love

Love is an amazing thing;
You will feel the sudden rush,
That burst of energy;
You know it used to be a crush,
But now it's more than that;
I feel something special;
You're the missing part of me;
The door inside and you're the key.

Keira Bettaney (12)
Edensor Technology College

Blackpool

I went to Blackpool with my family,
We saw the great Blackpool Tower.
I felt like I had all the power,
To reach every big tower.

The beach was beautiful for all to see,
The donkeys were as determined as they could be,
The fair rides were furious, just as I thought,
My ticket to Blackpool was well bought.

Emma Ball (11)
Edensor Technology College

Rainbows!

A rainbow is a present sent,
By a little leprechaun,
I saw it while I was mowing the lawn,
The colours were amazing,
I stood there watching and gazing!

It had deep red,
Bright yellow,
Rosy pink,
Sunset-orange,
Plum-purple,
Sea-blue,
Nutmeg-brown,
Bluebell-violet,
And of course pea green,
It was all supreme!

I hope the rainbow has a pot of gold,
Then I could sell my old household!
I'd be rich, rich beyond my dreams!
I could even buy a limousine!
But the best treat is the one we see,
That's enough for you and me!

Abi Addison (11)
Ryecroft Middle School

People And The World

People are different all around,
Different sizes, colours and ages,
The history of slaves living in cages,
Fascinating is what we are,
Kings and modern guys in a bar,
Some are bad and some are good,
If you could change I know you would,
All the people around the world,
The ones in Australia have fish hurled,
Never will I see everything in the world,
If I did I'd end up twirled,
There are many countries, 195 to be precise,
Most countries eat lots of spice,
People say they've travelled it all,
But the world's too big and we're too small,
I would love to experience it myself,
But it would just end up as pictures on a shelf,
Everyone is completely different, all 6 billion of us,
So why's there the wars and all that fuss?
All in all the place is great,
Even to my best mate,
But for now I'll stay where I am,
And hopefully never will eat ham,
That's a poem about the world and the people in it,
But that's enough for me to know,
I barely know my brother Joe.

Samuel Tilbrook (11)
Ryecroft Middle School

Nature Needs Help

Think what we've got - forests miles long,
Parrots in trees singing their birdsong.

Beautiful lakes shining like a mirror in the sun,
There's a dolphin in the sea playing, having fun.

Little clownfish burrowing in the coral down at the bottom of the sea,
Kids running round and round following a buzzy bee.

Polar bears chasing hares over the ice,
Poor hare, that's not very nice.

Waterfalls splash and crash, foaming down the rocks,
Grizzly bears catch salmon as they drop in their frocks.

Knock, knock, do you know nature needs help?
Who cares? Not me, don't you see I can't help?

Think; forests get cut down, parrots are scared,
Lakes are black with oil, fishermen are scared.

Dolphins, clownfish are dying, kids are crying
Polar bears, no hares to chase, they're all dying.

Waterfalls too polluted for salmon to swim.

It's a disaster, how can I help just the little things?

Rebecca Callear (11)
Ryecroft Middle School

The Weekend

Ah, the weekend, the lovely, lovely weekend,
Two whole days off school
And now I can play with my friend.
Now it's Saturday morning, now what should I do?
Breakfast? Lie in? I know, I'll do something new.
I'll go to Spar and buy some bread,
All those carbohydrates go straight to my head!
Saturday evening, The Simpsons is on,
Oh no it's half-past eleven, where has the time gone?
Oh well, time to go to bed, see you in the morn,
I'm up on Sunday and just at the break of dawn.
I'll go play football with my mates in the park
Then I'll come home with my best mate Mark.
We'll have our tea, probably beans on toast,
We just might have the rare, lovely lamb roast.
'See you Mark,' I say as he is on his way home.
'Goodnight Mum,' I yawn, going up the stairs.
'Mark!' shouts Mum, in the morning yelling, 'We're late!'
'Oh no!' I yelp, 'Is it Monday already?' running out the gate!

Ben Lamburn (11)
Ryecroft Middle School

Shopping!

Yesterday I went shopping for lots of things,
Food, books and even bling.
I stayed there till four in the afternoon,
I really do like it, you know, Jordan's new perfume!

I bought make-up, shoes and even toys,
I'll keep them for my two little boys.
I used my credit card that has a lot of money,
For my mum I even bought a jar of honey.

I went to Primark and bought some new clothes,
I went into Boots and bought nail varnish for my new pink toes.
When I got back I went to the vets,
Only to pick up my two new pets.

When I got home I put up my feet,
As my shopping trip was complete.
I went upstairs to start to get ready,
Although I realised I had loads of time so I could be steady!

Leigh-Ann Spruce (11)
Ryecroft Middle School

Music

We all like songs
Some are really wrong
Others are really dancey
More are very prancey.

Music can be happy
Music can be sad
Music when it's your birthday
It's the best you've ever had.

Music is all around us
From the church to the street
With the rhythm and blues
To the heavy metal beats.

Listen to your music
Whatever you like
And enjoy it from birth
For the rest of your life.

Georgia Chisholm (11)
Ryecroft Middle School

Friends

My friends mean a lot to me
We're the closest friends there ever could be
We're always there together
And always smiling whatever the weather.

Well there's Georgia, Milli, Sadie, Holly and Leigh-Ann
Not forgetting Jess, Tamsin, Olivia and Rhian.

And there are loads more
I just don't have time to say.

But I'd better just write them
Or they will want me to pay!

Well Sam and Arron, Bethany and Harry
All act like my uncle Larry.

I love all my friends
Even when they do drive me round the bend.

Louisa Kelly (11)
Ryecroft Middle School

Derby's Football Game

Bywater was crying as his team were dying
And had to shout about the defence.
The manager who bought the pitch
Knew that he was really rich.

The ball bounced really high,
They needed a player tall and sly,
The crowd waved as the ball was saved.
There was a hole in the goal that made a threat.

The crowd shouted,
Someone was biting a pie at the top of the stadium
Sky high.
Someone was injured,
The crowd -
Hating and waiting
For the match to begin again.

Alex Hulme (11)
Ryecroft Middle School

Football

Rooney has the ball,
He passes to Crouch who is so tall,
They all walk onto the pitch,
With Ronaldo who's so rich.

The crowd chants a song,
As Rory Delap throws really long,
The crowd does the Mexican wave,
Because David Beckham has had a shave.

Alex Ferguson is chewing gum,
A tubby guy pats his tum,
The pie shop's closed,
Because everyone is looking at Victoria Beckham's pose.

Someone throws a can
And down goes a man.

Mathew Kent
Ryecroft Middle School

Food, Food

Food, food, wonderful food
Wonderful, wonderful, wonderful food
Turkey, turkey worldwide
Chicken, chicken lovely fried.

Food, food, wonderful food
Wonderful, wonderful, wonderful food
Cake, cake, it gets people awake
Jelly, jelly fills my belly.

Food, food, wonderful food
Wonderful, wonderful, wonderful food
Pie, pie heaven, food in the sky
Rice, rice, it tastes so nice.

Food, food, sense and touch, oh food
Food, I love so much.

Alex Saul (11)
Ryecroft Middle School

When I Was Bullied

I was once bullied,
It was really bad.
And when he called me 'Shorty',
It made me really mad.

When I played football,
And when I missed a shot.
He was always waiting,
With a terribly nasty plot.

And when it was the end,
I was quite relieved.
At least I thought it was the end
That's what I believe.

And when I came to school,
The very next day.
At break time I fell over,
He was in my way!

I asked him nicely,
'Why don't you go away?'
He replied gruntingly,
'It is my birthday!'

And now two years later,
I have been relieved,
And to be honest,
I'm glad that I believed!

Edward Irvine (11)
St Joseph's College, Trent Vale

Me!

When I'm unhappy I'm very sad
But when I'm happy I'm very mad.
All the time I have different feelings
And all of them for different meanings.

Maria Hanley (11)
St Joseph's College, Trent Vale

Adults Vs Teens: The War Of Crime

'Crime everywhere,' they say.
'This young generation, when will it end?'
But can they be sure it's our fault?
A part of the problem is their own!
They are guilty.
Too much hating, give peace.
'Too much crime and evil in children,' they say.
'We blame it on them,' I say,
For in so many cases, it's sad but it's true.
The title 'delinquent' fits older folk too.

This is what most teens think,
It's the old folks who go and drink,
They're the ones who cause the fuss,
They're the ones who shout and cuss.

So stop this nonsense now!
Please stop it now!

Luca Stone (11)
St Joseph's College, Trent Vale

The World That I Live In

This is the world that we live in,
Why don't we keep it young?
'Cause this is the world that we live in,
Why do we chop it down?
How would you like it done to you?
Think of the animals, think of the trees.
The sky that gives us a breeze,
Because this is the world that we live in,
Why make things extinct?
This is the world that we live in.
I'm tired of global warming, of extinction and all things bad.
But people don't understand,
What are they doing, soon,
Yes soon, the world will freeze,
That will teach you a lesson.

Christopher Webb (11)
St Joseph's College, Trent Vale

Dreams Make You Grow Up Fast

Once, long, long ago, I had my first dream
About buttercups and daisies, tulips and roses
All alongside a stream.

Not long after, after the first, I had another dream
About raining cats and dogs and a rat that married a hog!
Plus a banshee that thought she could sing,
And a bug that swallowed a ring!
Then the disaster struck me, a terrible event happened
I grew up, and no longer had these dreams.
But then, I thought to myself:
Everyone has to grow up at one point
And today is my point, whether I like it or not.
It is for the best that I become a grown adult
And so you should too.

Tiana Deakes (11)
St Joseph's College, Trent Vale

It's Boring!

It makes me feel sick.
I'd much rather be playing on the Wii,
Or stuffing my face with crisps or chocolate is a good feeling to me.

Thursday is the most boring day of all,
As double English, followed by double maths is sure not a treat.
A double chocolate sundae afterwards sounds a better choice to me!

The best day of all is Saturday,
As I go shopping all day with my friends,
Parent and teacher free zone, but I always tell myself never speak too soon
As I bump into one or the other almost every week!

Sunday is cool as well as I can mess about,
I can lie down and sleep in till, say, one or two o'clock!
Then I need to get ready for the next day. School! *Argh!*

Lucy Deakin (11)
St Joseph's College, Trent Vale

I Am What I Am!

Calling me ugly won't make you beautiful.
Calling me dumb won't make you clever.
Calling me fat won't make you thin.
Calling me a loner won't make you popular.
Calling me small won't make you tall.
Calling me quiet won't make you chatty.
Calling me weak won't make you strong.

I am what I am for a reason.
That reason is:
God made me like this.
I have friends because they like my personality.
My family loves me the way I am.
We are all different for a reason.

Abbi Fearns (11)
St Joseph's College, Trent Vale

Emotions

I'm finding it strange,
But you don't know what I'm feeling,
I'm trying not to show it,
But I'm feeling very sad,
I don't know what to do,
I'm trying to be happy,
But I can't; everything is sad,
And suddenly I'm free,
Sadness is now happiness,
I'm feeling so joyful, I feel I could fly,
Nothing can change this, I am who I am,
My emotions are free with me.

Joseph Powell (11)
St Joseph's College, Trent Vale

The World I Live In

Just because I don't fight, doesn't mean I'm weak.
Just because I'm not the party kind, doesn't mean I can't hang out.
Just because I'm clever, doesn't mean I'm a nerd.
Just because all the staff like me, doesn't mean I'm a teacher's pet.
Just because I'm quiet, doesn't mean I don't speak up for what I believe in.
Just because I walk away, doesn't mean I'm a chicken.
Just because I think before I act, doesn't make me a loser.

I am who I am and this is who I shall be forever.
Like me or don't that's your choice.
Accept me for who I am.
God made me how I am.

Hasnain Mazhar (12)
St Joseph's College, Trent Vale

Random Feelings

I am sitting on my garden wall staring at the squashed football.
The moon is like a peace of cheese
I feel like grabbing it and giving it a good squeeze.
My mum keeps shouting at me to come and get my tea
But I don't want to because my cat has fleas.
I feel a trickle down my back
Now my mum will give me a good smack.
My mum shouts me again
But I feel another pain.

Naomi Ball (11)
St Joseph's College, Trent Vale

Contrast

Happy, sad, friendly, mad,
I'll always feel one of these,
But where I go, I'll try to show,
Happiness instead of being mad.

When I'm excited, when I am glad,
When I am hiding under my hat,
Try to remember, even in December,
That sometimes I can be mad.

Thomas Mitchell (11)
St Joseph's College, Trent Vale

White Witch

Her cloak billows out in a flurry of white,
She doesn't know if her decision is right,
Pacing and thinking, then pacing some more,
Her sheet of blonde hair is brushing the floor,
For this great woman has done a great crime,
So big that it cannot be fit in a rhyme,
But I will tell you, as you would tell me,
The white witch is evil and all need to see.

The mass stealing started a month before now,
I can see you asking, 'Why?' and 'How?'
Well I give you the answer that will shake your core,
The white witch cooks humans to stick on her floor,
To decorate her floor, to make it look right
For her black witch friends who are visiting tonight
And they cackle with laughter at the effort they see,
'Aren't you still hungry? That's all you had for tea?
That's real compassion to kill so very few!
I'd have ten every night if I were you!'
So now you know that if mates disappear,
The white witch is hovering around, so near,
Be careful in day, be careful at night,
So when on TV, there's disappearances galore,
You know those poor people are on the white witch's floor.

Tyra Anglin (12)
St Margaret Ward RC High School, Stoke-on-Trent

One Night, One Future

One look, one touch,
One word too much,
I stare at you,
Magnificence plus two,
I send a drink, whatever you like,
Do you believe in love at first sight?
I feel my heart beating so fast,
To the sound of your voice I hear at last,
For the first time I look in your eyes,
I want you forever, one rule, no lies,
Your hand on mine, our legs so tight,
You reach in by the look of a light,
Our lips touch, our eyes shut,
Within seconds it's time to wake up,
Butterflies in my tummy ache,
While the thought of love I make.
You never know you could be the one,
Make this last for all we know, come tomorrow you could be gone.
Romance, passion.
Love can happen,
A petal from a rose,
That's someone I have chosen,
Mine forever,
Forever together,
A scent of perfume lingering off your neck.
Move in with me, I will have to check,
I send you chocolates, I send you flowers,
I win you over with all my powers,
One promise you have to make,
Don't leave me when I awake,
Two words you have to say,
Three letters stand in the way,
I do, you've said it now, declared your love for me,
We've done it now, you've made me complete, all this time
You held the key.

Hollie Embury (14)
St Margaret Ward RC High School, Stoke-on-Trent

They Told Me

They told me
If I did it
I would fit in
But if I drank it
I'd commit a sin

If I put it down my throat
It could make me happy
So then I did
What I did
I grabbed the bottle
And unscrewed the lid

They told me
If I did it
I could stick around
Give it a sniff
I could fall to the ground

The fumes go up
Up through your nose
A little cough
A pat on the back
Just wish they'd cut me
A little slack

They told me
If I did it
I could be their friend
Put that smoke in my mouth
It could be the end

That tube in my mouth
Would shorten my life
So I went into town
Saw the guys where
They were stood
Grabbed the cigarette
Off them
And stuck up my hood

They told me
If I did it

I would be one of the crowd
But then I put my
Foot down
And made myself proud

I will stand up
And make myself happy
Because I want to enjoy
My life
I won't go around
Ruining it with a knife.

Joely Frain (12)
St Margaret Ward RC High School, Stoke-on-Trent

Paper Pressure

The time comes nearer,
My heart beats faster like the sound of a siren.
This is because today I have my first exams . . .

As the bell rings my body leaps with shock,
And I start to think of what might happen.
I say to myself:
What happens if I go wrong?
What happens if I do good?
What happens if I succeed but still get called a nerd?
What happens if I sit there thinking like a lost and confused bird?

But one thing I know for sure,
Is that if you try hard you won't have to endure,
Just do your best,
Like all the rest,
And then being a teenager is not such a bore.
Instead of that you will just have to adore.

Listen to me now,
Listen to me once,
If you can believe,
You can achieve,
Then you can be the pilot of your own life!

Sophia Naeem (12)
St Margaret Ward RC High School, Stoke-on-Trent

It's My Life

He says, 'I want it.'
He says, 'Give it a go.'
He tries it on a lot,
But I just say no.

My friends say it's good,
Every once in a while,
They often say too,
It gives you an edgy style.

Apparently, it's cool to drink,
But you just end up sick.
All this underage drinking,
You'll end up in the nick.

I often think, *have they been caught?*
I mean, that is stealing.
They say it's great to get things free,
But that's not the way I feel.

Teenage years, they're not all that bad,
And I have lots more trouble heading my way.
But even though it's all true,
I have something to say.

I love my life as it is.
I love my friends, school, I love it all.
Lots of opportunities in teenage years,
It keeps me proud and tall.

I've felt lost when surrounded by friends,
But I've got to understand,
It's my life, I love it.
It's my life in my hands.

Olivia McIntyre (13)
St Margaret Ward RC High School, Stoke-on-Trent

My Answer To The World

If you were to ask me
How I feel
About the world
What we should do
And if science has all the answers
I'd say I don't know.

If the world is at an end
So be it
If we are the cause
You never know for sure
If it is natural
Then it's meant to be.

Science hasn't got all the answers
To the world
Not all questions
Can be answered.

As to what we should do
I'm not sure
I just do what I can
I do what I want
I don't live my life
Trying to save something
That has no hope
Or trying to protect
Myself from danger
I just live my life
The way I want to
And just that.

Christine Murimi (13)
St Margaret Ward RC High School, Stoke-on-Trent

Pre-Teen Problems

Tomorrow is my birthday
Soon I'll be thirteen
But just what kind of dismay
Is waiting to be seen?

Will my friends seem changed to me
Or will they be the same?
Will they think that crime and drugs
Are just a funny game?

Or will it be the other way round?
Will the person that's changed be me?
Will I want to deal cocaine?
Or want to do sick graffiti?

Will people want to bully me
Because of the way I think?
Will all the rumours be round the school
Before I get a chance to blink?

My hips are getting wider,
I need to wear a bra.
Will all this sudden puberty,
Make everyone go ha-ha?

Adolescence seems torture, man,
I'm glad it doesn't last long.
If I'm right all my friends will
Soon be wearing a thong!

Regan Wain (12)
St Margaret Ward RC High School, Stoke-on-Trent

The Day I Saw My Favourite Band

I look around, I see the bright lights.
People of all ages jumping up and down.
The music is blaring, silence is no more.
People are walking around selling ice cream,
Candyfloss and much, much more.
This is the day I will remember forever more!

Natasha King (11)
St Margaret Ward RC High School, Stoke-on-Trent

Someone's Watching Over Me

Devastation, heartbreak, relief!
That bug in your heart burning yet somehow now it's twisted.
How to feel?
The pain she was living is dead
But so is my world, my rock, my inspiration.
How to feel?
The wondering, the not knowing, the waiting has ended.
But the looking back, the missing it, the pulling chains of my heart have just begun.
How to feel?
Tears of looking forward, the devilish fear of that day tearing your sanity apart is over.
But the tears of wanting her back flood my now less glinting eyes and boulder down my face.
How to feel?
Her pain has gone.
But the pain in my family's less rose-red faces and the way my brother tries to smile collapses my nearly bursting heart.
How to feel?
I've lost my mummy, my mother, my guide.
But I've gained a guardian angel, a fairy godmother, a princess always by my side.
How to feel?
I know I can't feel the hug of love that raises the mountains in your heart and dismisses all hard feelings.
I know someone's watching over me!

Sophia Jayne McGough (15)
St Margaret Ward RC High School, Stoke-on-Trent

Ring Of Fire

Jumping through fire, the thrill of the heat.
The pedals under my feet send a shooting vibration straight up my legs.
The thrill of jumping through the fire makes you do it again and again.
Jumping through the fire, doing bar turns, landing on the floor,
Almost falling off my bike, doing cancans off the forest jump,
Also putting my life on the line.

Benjamin Bennett (11)
St Margaret Ward RC High School, Stoke-on-Trent

My Colourful Interpretations

Red
The colour of love
The colour of hate.

Orange
The colour of fire
The colour of flowers.

Yellow
The colour of sunshine
And of decay.

Green
The colour of envy
And nature.

Blue
The colour of calm
And stormy seas.

Purple
The colour of bruises
And of remembrance.

Colours signify
So much
And yet so little.

My colourful interpretations
Just like words . . .

Chloe Frances Roberts (15)
St Margaret Ward RC High School, Stoke-on-Trent

My Greatest Inspiration

I wanted to shout, to scream, to yell
About my greatest inspiration.
But then suddenly, my smile fell . . .
My face went blank
My heart then sank
What, oh what should I do?

Bethany Perkin (15)
St Margaret Ward RC High School, Stoke-on-Trent

Drugs And Smoking

A drug is a bind,
It limits your mind,
You cannot get rid of it once it's there,
Oh, how you wish you had stuck to the juice of a pear,
As you whine
About how you've had too much wine,
You think: *isn't worth the benefits,*
Although, are there any that fit?

Avoiding drugs is about strength,
And doing so means going to any length.
So long as you avoid it,
You are safe from every hit.
The same as avoiding smoking,
It can make you a king,
That is, if you can avoid that suicide,
And don't join the smoking side.

Smoking kills and yet is seen as 'cool'
But when they are dead will they rule?
Smoking should be against the law,
Particularly as the amount of people dying of it
Is becoming more and more.
Smokers think they are clever,
But they won't be forever!
I would rather live in Hell
Than put up with a smoker's smell.

Roman Huczok (12)
St Margaret Ward RC High School, Stoke-on-Trent

What I Am

I am an eagle silently stalking my prey and then swooping down
and taking its life
I am a raging storm, aggressive but controlled.
I am the slickest jet in the skies, skilfully manoeuvring through the skies.
I am the Empire State Building, high in the sky, standing proud.

I am an eagle, soaring through the electric blue sky.

Zac Humphreys
St Margaret Ward RC High School, Stoke-on-Trent

Alexander

What I did almost cost him his life
The very thing haunts me
In the deepest part of my soul
The tree that I pulled him out
Cackles at me with malicious whirls.

Mother and Father
Scream and run
Comfort him from near death
Grandmother and Grandfather
Shame me for my insolence
The gift bestowed on me
Of a little brother; almost thrown to the ashes.

Luck had no role in this
For God knew his time had not come
The angels had come down and cushioned his fall
A feeling of relief overwhelmed me.

Coolness of ice soothed the injury
Tears still fell from the face
As Mother comforted him
And a grandmother glared
As I sat in the corner unable to speak.

What I did almost cost him his life
But God had other plans
For my little brother's time had not come.

Aaron Antrobus (16)
St Margaret Ward RC High School, Stoke-on-Trent

Snow

Snow is white as you
And me too, fun to do
But we have to wait.

The school is shut, it is
Too much for Mum and Dad,
My mum tells me to go have a snowball fight.

Leon Austin (11)
St Margaret Ward RC High School, Stoke-on-Trent

Jennifer: I Miss You

Nervously hovering at the bus stop, awaiting the spluttering engine and
jeering hiss of the brakes.
Flash my pass, a quick fake smile, stumble up the stairs; keep
looking down.
The violent engine shakes me over the hard, cracked road, jerking as the
bus struggles up that steep hill . . . almost impossible to climb.
One of those big things, you know? That you just can't climb.
Just can't get over - it almost kills you trying . . . no end, no horizon, just a
steep, dark road.
Arriving at school, keep looking down.
Don't let your red stinging eyes drown.
Round the back of the gym, stumbling and tripping over my own
feet - blinded by tears.
Down the steps, keep looking down; barge through the crowd.
An overpowering sea of angry waves, foaming and dragging me even
further under.
No one understands or cares.
No one realises, yet one in three people experience it.
Imagine just for a second, how many people are crippled with the feeling of
losing someone, yet everyone is so wrapped up in their own lives.
'Why is she crying again?' they snigger.
I don't want much; I don't have much anymore,
I just want their eyes to leave me.
Surrounded by people; I'm alone.

Katie Johnson (15)
St Margaret Ward RC High School, Stoke-on-Trent

Football

I'm happy when I play football
I'm sad when I play football

I'm happy when I score
I'm sad when they score

I'm happy when I win
I'm sad when they win.

This is why I play football.

Cameron Fryer (12)
St Margaret Ward RC High School, Stoke-on-Trent

Teenage Years

Teenage years, the so-called worst of your life,
Like heavy rain falling from the sky.
I, in the middle of all,
I, feel like time is going so slow.

They say I have to take drugs,
I, say no
They say it's cool
I, say why?

Why is having underage sex so cool?
Why is smoking cool?
Why is bullying others cool?
They stand in silence with nothing to say.

I, say look forward to the future,
I, say look forward to leaving those school doors when school's finished.
With friends who care for you.

There's no need to be scared, anxious, confused and depressed.

Being a teenager does not last forever,
So make sure you live these times happily.
You are you, no one else is you.

Keith Maramba (12)
St Margaret Ward RC High School, Stoke-on-Trent

This Is Me

I am a roaring lion, thrashing through the bushes.
I am a hailstorm cutting your pathetic, weak skin.
I am a green spotlight, blinding your weak eyes.
I am a helicopter, spying on you from above.
I am Saturday, giving you a rest.
I am a pair of socks, protecting your feet and providing warmth.
I am a bed, relaxing you completely.
I am a tree, for you to climb.
I am the Empire State Building, giving you a view.
I play rock music, rocking your world to bits.
I am me.

Siobhan Toft (11)
St Margaret Ward RC High School, Stoke-on-Trent

Something About Sofia

She lives in a dream
More dazzling than friction

Imaginary yet real
She defies all prediction

An incredible girl
Sofia draws you right in

To where the everyday ends
And magic begins . . .

Laugh with me . . .

Her playful wink
And mischievous smile

The flirtatious side
Of her innocent style

No thought or worry
Of what's meant to be

First laughter, then love
. . . along came she.

Samreen Khan
St Margaret Ward RC High School, Stoke-on-Trent

Reflection

Go on my darling - you can do it
A smile that could light up a thousand eyes
A laugh that could wake up a thousand minds
A heart that could inspire a thousand souls
A cry that could soften a thousand lives

A sun that could lift a thousand thoughts
A hand that could calm a thousand cries
A life that could love a thousand loves

A love that is eternal
A night that is forever
And a death.

Ellen Madden (16)
St Margaret Ward RC High School, Stoke-on-Trent

Me And My Friend

Me and you have been through moments that were happy and sad.
After that we don't feel so bad.

We have fun, we stick together,
We are best friends, friends forever.

Me and you always share,
I think we're always fair.

People like us never call anyone names,
But we fight like real hot flames.

I think you're really funny,
I'd never call you a bunny.

Me and you have never been told
That you are silver and I am gold.

I think you are bright
Even though I gave you a fright.

I'd like to say,
That with you I'd love to play.

Jessica Ann Dunn
St Margaret Ward RC High School, Stoke-on-Trent

Teenage Life

7 years of traumatic teenage life.
Lots of things happen like zits, drink or even a wife.
My dad says, 'Make the most of it and try to do your bit
To prove to people these years ain't so bad
When they say they are hard and sad.'
I want to do the best that I can
And try not to get an ASBO ban.
I will try not to drink and smoke,
I won't take drugs like heroin or coke.
I will make the best of this amazing time
And will never get put down by silly crimes.
So now I know these years ain't so bad,
So make the most of it because you'll be glad.

Alexander Manning (12)
St Margaret Ward RC High School, Stoke-on-Trent

Choke

Intent, glum faces staring
Itching for release
Their only option is you
You take the stage.

Gasping, squinting, hoping . . .
Relief as the recognisable blaze bell echoes in your head
Their eyes widen
Eyebrows crease
Necks subside.

You open your mouth
Dry gums, itchy throat . . . empty head
'Hello I'm . . .'
Your heart pounds
Choke!

Well if that man in the front row can come in shiny red pants . . .
'Howard'
'I'm here to talk about how pointless stage fright is . . .'

Rebecca Steventon (15)
St Margaret Ward RC High School, Stoke-on-Trent

The Starlight

There it was, on that Saturday night
Glistening and gleaming at such a height
I wondered and wondered at what it could be
So tempting it was, to go out and see
I couldn't stop looking at that gorgeous sight
Gleaming all lonely, on that Saturday night
So many pictures dancing round in my head
Of that wonderful thing seen, before going to bed
I had to see it again, I knew it was right
To see its colours, so golden and bright
It just happened I didn't see it again
So I decided to give it a spectacular name
That thing I saw, on Saturday night
I gave the name of Starlight.

Megan Zdrodowski (11)
St Margaret Ward RC High School, Stoke-on-Trent

As I See Her Growing Up

She stands aside watching,
Amazed at what she sees.
A fragile image of herself,
The offspring of her seed.

Her little girl is growing fast,
Already starting school.
The first days are the hardest,
For Mum to play it cool.

Anxiety at separation,
Most common, so they say.
For a mum it's even harder,
To give her child away.

Before she knows a year has passed,
Her child is now afoot.
Loving, learning, listening, loud,
To follow up all dreams.

Holly Pearce (11)
St Margaret Ward RC High School, Stoke-on-Trent

Shadows Of Vengeance

As soon as the shadows move across my face,
I can't find an ending any place.
It made my friend dead,
It chopped off his head.
All in his comfy little bed.
What am I to do?
I can't start anew,
It's no longer me and you!
You're the demons in my life,
Why do we always carry a knife?
Yes, it's me, I will dissemble no more,
I won't look through the door.
I admit the deed,
I don't smoke weed.
But I ended his life! I stopped the beating of his hideous heart.

Sam King (13)
St Margaret Ward RC High School, Stoke-on-Trent

Chocoholic

Eat some chocolate,
Just me and you.
To fill us up,
And share some too.

Let's eat some chocolate,
Just you and me.
Chocolate for breakfast,
Chocolate for tea.

Let them eat some chocolate,
Just that group of four.
Like us they love chocolate,
And want some more.

I need to go,
I'm craving for the bad.
That chocolate holds,
It's making me mad!

Devon Bennett (11)
St Margaret Ward RC High School, Stoke-on-Trent

People

People are different in different ways.
People like different plays.
People love football and different sports
Or basketball courts.

Girls like make-up some may not,
Some may like it in different spots.
Girls like boys more than others,
I bet they take after their mothers.

Boys like girls, maybe not,
Some may love girls a lot.
Boys like sports or even bikes,
Some may go on very long hikes.

People are different than others.

Brittanee Swindells
St Margaret Ward RC High School, Stoke-on-Trent

Say No! Say Yes!

Say no to drinking,
Say no to drugs,
Say no to smoking,
Just do what you should.

Say no to the bullies,
Say no to pressure.
Say no to vandals,
Just get the right measure.

Say yes, be healthy,
Say yes, be safe,
Say yes to respect,
Just show your face.

Say yes, be friends,
Say yes, be brave.
Say yes to school,
And we're not all the same.

Katie Brown (12)
St Margaret Ward RC High School, Stoke-on-Trent

Even Though

Even though I don't drink,
Do drugs, smoke or swear,
It doesn't mean I'm stupid,
Just that I'm very aware.
Aware of what they can do to you,
And how dangerous they can be,
Because when you're old and forgetful,
I'm sure you will agree
That drugs and alcohol are stupid,
And smoking's pointless you see!
So take a leaf out of my book,
And stop now whilst you can,
Because in years to come you'll regret it,
And wonder why you ever began.

Rachel Lawton (12)
St Margaret Ward RC High School, Stoke-on-Trent

Bully Or Victim?

If you're being bullied,
Show that you don't care,
They'll leave you if they don't see you run,
But they will still be quite a scare.

They will make you feel less of yourself,
Sad, depressed and weak,
They show their point through violence,
And they never last just a week.

Act like you're ignoring them,
Act like you don't care,
Act like they're not there at all,
Pretend that they're just floating in the air.

Bullying is a really big problem,
And it can happen at any time,
You're either the bully or the victim, but remember,
The bully always ends up with a life of crime.

Daniel Davenport (12)
St Margaret Ward RC High School, Stoke-on-Trent

The Best PE Excuse Of All

On a cold winter's day, near the car park of staff,
Mr Anslow: 'Do multi-gym . . .' Huh! Don't make me laugh,
My head was afire as a weight struck my chest,
My complaining skills could be put to the test,
I flew to the floor like a trickle of tears,
To a chorus of laughter from my hideous peers,
I flailed and I wailed on the sweat-stained floor,
My thrashing around had left me so very raw,
The gremlins who watched thought it was a joke,
But I knew within seconds I was having a stroke,
The ambulance men whisked me off of my feet,
Their notorious probes left me well and truly beat,
But I am still happy, as I take my last breath,
For I have the best PE excuse of all . . . death.

Adam Bakewell (15)
St Margaret Ward RC High School, Stoke-on-Trent

Teenage Life

Teenage life is not the best,
But not as bad as it may seem,
Getting pushed around and told you're a pest.
Getting told off because you're being mean.

People think it's all about smoking and drugs
But I think they're a pain.
But not all teenagers are total thugs,
We're not all quite insane.

My exams are coming up soon,
This will determine what I am when I'm older.
Walking in school my mum's hand on my shoulder,
I look like a right buffoon.

I'll pass a pretty girl I like soon,
I totally hide my head,
I'm so embarrassed, my face goes red.
So I run into the exam room.

Josh Tyler (12)
St Margaret Ward RC High School, Stoke-on-Trent

Poison

He's just like poison
Spreading quickly through time
But he whispers that it's fine
How can something so deadly feel so right?
It's winning, defeating, no point trying to fight
I'm trembling
I'm falling
As he wraps himself around my veins
But still, even now, there is no pain
I have become so numb
Yet he's pumping like a drum
I can't stop this from happening to me
There isn't a feeling like being free
He's just like poison.

Samantha Stubbs (15)
St Margaret Ward RC High School, Stoke-on-Trent

The Accident

No one saw it coming,
The phone call one afternoon
That changed our lives forever,
They said that it happened too soon.
He didn't see the car
As he had taken the corner wide
And flew from the seat of his motorbike,
Landing by its side.
And the woman behind the wheel,
Shaking as she cried,
Ran from her ruined vehicle,
And held him where he died.
And everyone always said,
That if he had dropped his keys
Or turned around to say,
A final goodbye to his wife and child
Would he still be here today?

Olivia Waring (15)
St Margaret Ward RC High School, Stoke-on-Trent

My Weird Day!

One day I had PE, we had trampolining, it was really fun,
Until I flung off and really hurt my bum.
The ambulance came just in time,
because I thought I was going to die,
When we got to the hospital, I was screaming and shouting,
but all I really wanted was a red skittle.
A weird man came and injected me
with a needle the size of Jupiter,
I think I got stupider.
Finally I got to go home, went to pick up my mobile phone,
but arrived home.
I opened the door and my crutches fell to the floor.
I got a big fright, then we partied all night.

Tamika Wilson (12)
St Margaret Ward RC High School, Stoke-on-Trent

Our Glorious Dead

The Germans are strong,
They break through our ranks killing,
I've lost my best friend.

Bang, bang, bang you hear
Men screaming out for help, *bang*,
But now we are late.

We are leaving today,
Leaving our dead,
It is a sad day for us.

We hold our heads high,
We win . . . but have lost loads of men,
We are nearly home.

We march into more trouble,
But we keep winning,
Marching for our country.

Daniel Johnson (13)
St Margaret Ward RC High School, Stoke-on-Trent

It's Breakfast Time!

It's a new day,
All fresh and all clean,
My tummy's rumbling,
Cuz breakfast time is here,
Hmm should I have
Coco Pops or toast,
Or maybe should I finish
Yesterday's Sunday roast?
Hmm should I have
Eggs scrambled?
I better hurry up,
Cuz I've got to ramble,
I have chosen my meal
After such a big deal . . .

And now I'm full.

Tanisha Kent (11)
St Margaret Ward RC High School, Stoke-on-Trent

Empty

The shining needle of an aeroplane trails white thread
through the cerulean fabric of the sky.
A dog barks at a stranger.
My heart twists itself out of my chest;
Fifty miles away, an old man stares at an empty chair.

A cascade of water tumbles from the gutter to the pavement.
The yawning chasm of pain widens itself in front of me.
A mother without a mother stares into the emptiness
full of memories.

You can stop all the clocks if you want to, but life goes on.
Not life in particular, just that grotesque leviathan
that is life in general.
Not her life.

A coarse squalling mass wheels over the school: vultures circle.
A plain grey slab marks the place where there aren't any memories.

Eleanor Grigson
St Margaret Ward RC High School, Stoke-on-Trent

Pat The Gangster Cat

There once was a cat whose name was Pat, he was a guard
Forever and ever armed, with guns and a crow bar
And he used to show off with his fancy car
Mugging people all through the night until the bright morning light
Roaming round in his shiny car, until the tyres got stuck in tar
He pushed his car up the road
But then he saw a green toad, the toad said, 'Hi, how are you?'
The cat said, 'Go away! I don't need to talk to you!'
Pat killed someone that very night
He ran off and left the murder scene, leaving no evidence where he had been
Before time he realised he shouldn't have committed this awful crime
But that night
He was killed in a cat fight
Pat didn't wake up but his eyes closed tight
He wasn't going to wake up in the morning light!

Jessica Booth (11)
St Margaret Ward RC High School, Stoke-on-Trent

I Know, I Understand, I Believe

I know I might not be liked very much.
I understand how sometimes people say mean things.
I believe in some rumours that may hurt people.
I know I might give in to peer pressure now and again.
I understand how sometimes people are seriously damaged by it.
I believe in myself to never pressure anyone.
I know how to say, 'No!'
I understand how rejecting offers can be hard.
I believe in the consequences of peer pressure.
I know I can turn my life around if it goes down the wrong path.
I understand people will say things to make me want to give up.
I believe in myself to love life and not to damage it.
I know, I understand and I believe!

Susan Machin (12)
St Margaret Ward RC High School, Stoke-on-Trent

My Dad

My dad is the best,
My dad has black hair,
I love my dad,
My dad is cool,
My dad works in the army,
He is the best in the world,
My dad is the sun,
My dad is the snow,
My dad loves me!
And I love my dad
My dad is the best,
My dad is cool,
My dad is my dad.

Aimee Ansell (11)
St Margaret Ward RC High School, Stoke-on-Trent

Random

Gliding golden eagle soaring slowly,
Shiny gold slowly melting,
Cool shoes can run quickly,
Red sofas slowly slump,
Stupid Simpsons sing sloppily,
Minty May moves delightfully,
Whistling winds sneak coolly,
Standing bridge arched cautiously,
Heated curry steams crazily,
Picturesque Alaska booms lovely,
Terrible thorns strike poses,
Thumping R'n'B blasts loudly,
That's my random poem.

Jackson Booth (13)
St Margaret Ward RC High School, Stoke-on-Trent

Friendship

My life is great
Around every corner I have a mate
It's good to have friends
Because they help you make amends
But sometimes they break your heart
And then you just fall apart
Sometimes they give you so much love
Just like all the feathers on a dove
I thought I knew my crew
Until they hit me faster than I knew
Always pick the right friends
Not the ones who think they're bad and cool
Because of their fashion trends.

Kasim Hussain (14)
St Margaret Ward RC High School, Stoke-on-Trent

My Mum

My mum is the sun
My mum is the rain
My mum is the snow
My mum tells me everything I want to know
My mum loves the guitar
My mum loves my grandad especially (RIP)
I love my mum, she's the best in the world!
She helps me with my homework
She cooks lovely food
She does all the hoovering
She is the best in the world
My mum has a family
My mum loves me!

Amy Dawson (11)
St Margaret Ward RC High School, Stoke-on-Trent

The Outside

I walk around, my head down
Keeping quiet, trying to hide
But when they come we all run
Running for our lives through the towns
Dodging trees and over walls
Staying away from the lights.

They catch us, we get beaten
Get thrown on the floor, punched and kicked
We protect ourselves, it's no use
They abandoned us, we have been beaten
I get on my feet, I'm OK
But my mates don't see another day.

William Beardmore (12)
St Margaret Ward RC High School, Stoke-on-Trent

I Was In Detention

I had a detention
It was all my fault
I got let out early
Because I put a bin together
So we can recycle
In a green bin

It was in English
And it was very
Boring because
I had to write
All homework must be handed in on time
Line by line.

Ryan Oliver Dale
St Margaret Ward RC High School, Stoke-on-Trent

Weather

The grey clouds hover over the house.
The rain patting louder than a large mouse.
Lightning bolts strike and light the sky,
Children run madly in to get dry.
The floor is wet, you slip and slide,
Children moan, no one else can go outside.

The sun has come out to shine today,
It is warm, the children play.
Rain is drying up, it sparkles in the sun,
Park is dry, ready to have fun.
Rises in the east, sets in the west,
This week to me will be the best.

Jennifer Sibley (11)
St Margaret Ward RC High School, Stoke-on-Trent

Homeless

I got thrown out when I was 15
By my parents, my family members when I was eating my Asian cuisine.
When the clock struck 1.00
I went to the don
And started selling drugs on the streets by the stream.
The streets, the streets are full of freaks.
When I was 20 I was lost and cold,
The don, my friends, left me on the road.
Stage one I started again,
Never trust a man who can never be your friend.
The streets, the streets are full of freaks.
The streets.

Qaseem Dastagheer (12)
St Margaret Ward RC High School, Stoke-on-Trent

Crime And Violence

Crime and violence is what some teenagers do,
Others don't, they put down their foot and shoe.
People think crime is cool,
Others think that they are a fool.
You may think that people who do crime are boring and bare,
Others do crime just for a dare.
All the graffiti, robbery and shoplifting, it's all lame,
But all you've got to think, is everyone the same?
Crime and violence are quite bad,
I know they could make you sad.
If only you were there and saw,
That not all teenagers break the law.

Giovanni Neglia (12)
St Margaret Ward RC High School, Stoke-on-Trent

My Dog

When my dog died I got very mad.
It also made me very sad
When my sheep dog got put down
It made me wear a great big frown
Later on I got another
It made me such a happy brother
The old Jemima was replaced by Maisie
And this dog is very crazy
The old dog never used to dig
But this would dig up twigs
The old dog never used a bed
But this one always rests her head.

Ross Leighton (12)
St Margaret Ward RC High School, Stoke-on-Trent

Best Friend

Today I found a friend,
My very best friend,
Her name's Tanisha,
A little princess.
She's like a flower,
One that's just bloomed,
Ant-like,
Small but strong,
Or maybe a ghost,
Whose spirit never dies.
What would I do if I didn't have her?
What would you do if you didn't have a friend?

Arlene Joy (11)
St Margaret Ward RC High School, Stoke-on-Trent

What Is My Favourite Sport?

Kick it, pass it, score a goal,
My favourite sport is football!

Bowl it, bat it, hit a six,
My favourite sport is cricket!

Scrummage, score a try, line out,
My favourite sport is rugby!

Boxing, tennis, golf,
Darts, bats and bowls,
Throwing, catching, caught.

I can't decide my favourite sport!

Kieran Greatrex (11)
St Margaret Ward RC High School, Stoke-on-Trent

Overlooked

If I did well in an exam, I bet no one would care
If I went out and vandalised something you'd hear it everywhere.

If I looked after a sick person's cat, I bet no one would care.
If I went and pulled a kid's hair, you'd hear it everywhere.

Not all teens are bad, not all are scary.
Not all wear black hoods and frighten old ladies.

So stop! Take a look at the good we can do,
We are young, we are smart, we are all as good as you.

So stop thinking 'bout the few that are bad,
Think instead of the good and be glad.

Hannah Clewes (12)
St Margaret Ward RC High School, Stoke-on-Trent

A Famous Man

There was once a famous man
Who was famous because of his van
He went to a prom, as famous people do
And found his love of his life
Jemma White.

4 years on in a church
With singer Alexandra Burke
A food fight started
The groom got hit
They were carted out of the church
Not forgetting Alexandra Burke.

George Billings (12)
St Margaret Ward RC High School, Stoke-on-Trent

All About Me

I am a hummingbird, singing gently among flowers.
I am the sun, shining down on the Earth.
I am the boldest orange catching people's eyes.
I am a private jet moving quicker than the wind.
I am the Saturday night boogie fever, performing with energy.
I am a pair of dance shoes practising constantly.
I am a mirror reflecting steps.
I am a supervisor, brighter than all flowers.
I am hip-hop, a style with a constant beat.
I am a theatre, comfortably entertaining people.

I am a performer . . .

Megan Hancock
St Margaret Ward RC High School, Stoke-on-Trent

On A Winter's Day

On a winter's day in a winter morning the birds
Outside my house were tweeting a song that
I longed for all morning. As I went downstairs
I got my bag on and off I went to school as I went
Through the door the winter air flowed past my face, it was
Cold and refreshing. I took my first breath and was
On my way. Through the gate out the street and into the
Field as I walked down the red robins were tweeting
And the sky was as white as a mouse. I kept walking onwards
Through the winter air, a tree had the same colour as my hair, there's
Nothing like the wonderful winter air.

Brandon Mutch
St Margaret Ward RC High School, Stoke-on-Trent

Untitled

I was sitting in the park,
When it all went dark,
And my old friend Mark,
His dog started to bark!

I went to the gate,
When I met my mate,
Who had just been on a date.

I went to get my favourite cake,
Which I loved to bake,
Then went to get some fishing bait.

Bradley Dawson & Jacob Cuthbert (11)
St Margaret Ward RC High School, Stoke-on-Trent

All About Me

I am a beautiful butterfly that flies high in the sky.
I only come out when it's sunny.
I am lime green, the biggest, brightest, boldest in the rainbow.
I am me.

Katie Louise Harley (11)
St Margaret Ward RC High School, Stoke-on-Trent

Community

C ool people and others, no one knows
O ver there is always a commotion
M oney is scarce everywhere
M aybe we need altogether community
U nity, community, that's what we need
N o one knows what has happened but the police are down
I n the fields, kids are drinking
T oo much fighting at night
Y ou and me can make it better by being a community

Every day, every night.

Chloe Ali Phillips (11)
St Margaret Ward RC High School, Stoke-on-Trent

Bike Tricks

Jumping in the mid-air
The air in my face
Doing none footers
With my body on the risk
Jumping in mid-air again and again
Every time doing different tricks
You name the trick
There isn't anything we can't do.
X up, Superman, bar tone, cancan, transfer and table top
We can do them all.

Joshua Barlow
St Margaret Ward RC High School, Stoke-on-Trent

Gymnastics

I love going to gymnastics
And doing routines on the beam
It's like nothing you've ever seen!
I love doing gymnastics
And doing routines on the floor
Forward rolls, cartwheels and lots, lots more.
I love going to gymnastics
And doing routines on the bar
I do my moves, I do them clean,
I love the bars, I am very keen.

Abigail Mannion
St Margaret Ward RC High School, Stoke-on-Trent

Who Am I?

I am a lion strolling softly through my territory.
I am sunny, bright and happy.
I am my bed, soft and comfortable.
I am a Lamborghini speeding through the countryside.
I am a Friday late night, no school the next day.
I am a fiery red burning as hot as the sun.
I am trainers, as soft as the soft leather.
I am bamboo, as hard as a rock.
I am the roar of Old Trafford.
I am the beat of R and B.

Thomas Hughes (11)
St Margaret Ward RC High School, Stoke-on-Trent

The Dark Princess

She roams the woods at nightfall, alone,
Casting dark spells, a shiver to the bone.
As swift as the wind she flies towards the light,
Making everything she passes mysteriously ignite.
Her gloomy castle looms in the dark,
Haunted trees set around it made of anything but bark.
Human skins cover her door,
To scare away young children who go wandering after boar.
So beware if you go for a walk alone,
The dark princess is watching for someone who dares moan.

Rebecca Smith (11)
St Margaret Ward RC High School, Stoke-on-Trent

Who Am I?

I am a tiger roaring at everyone
I am sunny every day but sometimes I rain
I am sitting around painting the walls purple and red
I am a Bentley brumming everywhere
I am Friday, the best day of the week
I am a dress showing off my beauty
I am a computer playing with my friends
I am bluebells I smell so nice
I am a skyscraper I'm so tall
I am soft music, so calm when I want to be.

Amy Bishop (12)
St Margaret Ward RC High School, Stoke-on-Trent

The Match

Balls flying in the air
Feet kicking everywhere
We rule the game.

After kick-off
A free kick is given
Brad takes his shot
The top corner it goes.

Cheers from the crowd
His dad looking proud.

Callum Thomas
St Margaret Ward RC High School, Stoke-on-Trent

Baby Sister

My baby sister, she's got her pink blanket,
My baby sister, she's got such small and little feet.
She has soft brown hair and sparkling blue eyes,
Every time I see her she makes my love rate rise.

She's only 5 weeks old and we've got a cold,
It makes me feel weak but her love gives me heat.
That's as sweet as a dove and a letter of love,
My baby sister, she's so tiny and cute.
That's my baby sister.

Joshua Jones (11)
St Margaret Ward RC High School, Stoke-on-Trent

Stars

Stars of the night,
Make the darkness bright,
Shining their light,
What a beautiful sight.

As I gaze at the sky you can see,
Just how high those stars are passing by,
Each one twinkling I spy.

Charlotte Gillon (11)
St Margaret Ward RC High School, Stoke-on-Trent

I Am Amazing

I am as soft as a rabbit.
I am as hot as the blazing sun.
I am as shiny as the one pound on the floor.
I am a relaxing Sunday morning.
I am a wet swimming costume all wet.
I am a TV seeing everyone.
I am a tall oak tree as high as the Empire State Building.
I am as big as the Stoke City stadium and I am popping everywhere like pop music.

Charlotte Hoskins (11)
St Margaret Ward RC High School, Stoke-on-Trent

What Am I?

I am a tiger racing through the leaves to catch my prey when I pounce.
I am the rain bouncing off the floor.
I am a fiery red burning through the Earth.
I am accelerating through all the streets.
I am Friday the end of the weekdays.
I am a comfy sofa to relax on.
I am a tree towering above everyone.
I am Old Trafford watching the games.
I am listening to R'n'B.

Dominic Hulme (11)
St Margaret Ward RC High School, Stoke-on-Trent

Moving Country

When I was eight I moved to England,
I went everywhere, met everyone,
I was happy, I was sad,
All I wanted was to go home.

In September 2006 I moved to Burslem,
Haven't moved away from there yet,
The next day it was my birthday.
Soon it was time to go to school.

Paulina Kurstak (12)
St Margaret Ward RC High School, Stoke-on-Trent

At High School

At high school you have got to stay cool,
Don't get your teacher's attention,
Because you might get detention,
At St Margaret Ward don't say you're bored,
At lunchtime
You get munch time,
You can go up to top pitch
And go up to the football pitch,
That's what I do sometimes.

Jessica Marquis (11)
St Margaret Ward RC High School, Stoke-on-Trent

First Day At School

The first day at school is always the worst.
It is all big and scary.
You can never find your way around.
And I'll tell you a secret,
School is not so bad when you find your toes.
PE I've got next.
I think that I have found my feet, have you?
I love school now, it is ever so fun
But don't forget your best buds.

Elliot Degg (11)
St Margaret Ward RC High School, Stoke-on-Trent

Why?

Why do people always judge us?
Why do we always get looked down on?
Why do people blame us?
Why is everyone scared of us?
Why has the world come to this?
Why are teenagers always the ones that cause riots?
Teenagers aren't the ones causing war.
So why blame us?

Ashlee Wallace (12)
St Margaret Ward RC High School, Stoke-on-Trent

This Is Me!

I am a tall, hairy monkey,
I am as bright as the sun,
I am as blue as the sky,
I am speeding through the sea like a yacht,
I am a relaxed Saturday,
I am a jacket that likes to keep warm,
I am as sweet as an orange tree,
I am as loud as a football stadium.
I have got the hit, the beat, the block of R'n'B.

Charlie Harding (12)
St Margaret Ward RC High School, Stoke-on-Trent

Just Because

Just because you don't do drugs,
Doesn't mean you're not cool.
Just because you don't smoke,
Doesn't mean you're a fool.
Just because you haven't had an achievement,
Doesn't mean you can't get one.
Just because you don't have many friends now,
Doesn't mean you can't get a ton!

Adnaan Ahmed (13)
St Margaret Ward RC High School, Stoke-on-Trent

Untitled

I am a quiet koala bear slouching hopelessly.
I am icy snow meandering smoothly.
I am a deep red maroon colour being splattered on the wall, shapelessly.
I am a hop-on tram, grabbing people urgently.
I am a useless Saturday trying to get people's attention badly.
I am a fluffy, cuddly, shrug wrapping for warmth, patiently.
I am an art deco armchair rocking gently.
I am a spider plant crawling down the wall gradually.

Jodie Yearsley (11)
St Margaret Ward RC High School, Stoke-on-Trent

I Am

I am a bird flying across the sky
I am the sun lighting the Earth
I am the pink covering people's clothes
I am the fastest jet flying so high in the sky
I am the Saturday night out dancing
I am a dress swaying across the dance floor
I am the most comfortable bed in the world.

Rejeanne Mae Gloria
St Margaret Ward RC High School, Stoke-on-Trent

A Smile

A smile is such a funny thing,
It wrinkles down your face,
And when it's gone you'll never find
Its secret hiding place,
You smile at one,
They smile at you,
Therefore one smile makes two.

Kayleigh Hogan (11)
St Margaret Ward RC High School, Stoke-on-Trent

Tiredness

Tiredness in your brain, saying goodnight,
The sun is going down in your head,
It is now time to say goodbye, don't put up a fight,
Go and jump in your nice warm bed.

Your bed is a warm, cosy black hole,
Be careful not to get lost in the masses of quilt,
And better still there is no toll,
Make sure you take off your kilt.

Now it's time to say goodnight,
And remember
Don't let the bed bugs bite!

Megan Pugh (11)
Stafford Grammar School

The Duet

Rosalie's long black hair mixed in the wind
With the short blonde hair of her new best friend.
Rosalie's skin was the colour of a chocolate bear
Whereas her friend Annie's was very fair.
In common they both only had one small thing,
The magic shine that their different eyes bring.
However, their friendship was nevertheless
Almost always perfect.

They sang at shows and dazed the crowds
And locked their different hands when they bowed,
They practised together every night
And their voices lit the rooms like a luminous light.
They felt they could do anything as long as they were together,
They thought their friendship and songs could last forever.
Little did they know what was about to happen
After the spectacular show.

After the show they did depart
Cheerfully and with joy in their hearts,
Until Rosalie reached home that day
And found a message to her dismay.
'Hi Rosalie, it's Annie, I'm going solo . . .
I got an incredible job offer in Soho!'
Rosalie thought their friendship would last forever
But that was before Annie left her.

Just then her bedroom mirror smashed
Like her unattainable dream crashed,
She was a feeble, lonely, innocent dove
Who was betrayed by the friend she loved.
In dismay she ran outside
To a bridge on the other side,
She looked at her reflection in the river one last time.
That day she fell asleep forever.

Anisah Haque (12)
Stafford Grammar School

Escaping

Why am I here? Why am I here?
Teeming with anger but most of all fear?
What is it that is so wrong with me,
That I am in this place I have to be?
I want to escape.

A Jew - am I the second class?
Do we always fail and never pass?
They keep us in this abomination,
With no way out of this camp of concentration.
I need to escape.

Everyone dies here, and we will too,
We don't deserve it - what's wrong with Jews?
Shooting all around me; die, die, die,
People disappearing like a rainbow in the sky.
I have to escape.

Need to get out, need to get out,
If we don't then there will always be doubt,
That the world will go on like this; not fair,
And not one person will ever care.
I will escape.

At the dead of night, we gather together,
With hopes that we will live on forever.
We creep out of our hut, and make a break,
Run, run, run, for goodness' sake!
I am escaping.

We reach the fence, and over we climb,
But then we know we're out of time.
A cacophony of gunshots and I go down,
I have no sight, no touch, no sound.
I was escaping.

Yasmin Duggal (12)
Stafford Grammar School

The Festive Season, Winter

The festive season, winter.
All is quiet, no rustling of animals,
In the frozen damp undergrowth,
Quite unlike the other months,
The festive season, winter.

The dark nights drawing in,
The early mornings just as dark,
It comes like a savage beast,
Invading the light,
The festive season, winter.

Brave men go out in their trucks,
Making us safe, they release salt,
They are soldiers that dissolve,
The always dangerous ice.
The festive season, winter.

The wonderful time of Christmas,
Children sending off their precious
Letters to the God-like Santa,
Finally the day has come,
The festive season, winter.

Children ripping open presents and
Screaming, 'He's come, he's come!'
The hot roast turkey and watery sprouts
Bubbling in the pot.
The festive season, winter.

The final countdown for 2010,
Your mom and dad drunk and
Falling about. Stay up till 12.00.
I love New Year's Eve.
The festive season, winter.

Samuel Carter (11)
Stafford Grammar School

The Ambition

There once was a boy named Jake,
Whose mother liked him to bake,
But playing the guitar was cool
And baking was made for a fool,
He wanted to impress his mates,
And he never ever got dates.

He bought a guitar, all silky and red,
But his mother called him to bake white bread,
He would plead and plead,
And plead and plead,
Until his mother finally gave in,
And threw the baking in the bin.

Four years later came Jacob's birthday
Which was conveniently placed in May,
May was the month of the talent show,
And it was a chance for him to glow,
About his newly found talent,
And to get onto the stage it took some gallantry.

Luckily for him a man from a group,
Was looking for a suit,
Of a fully professional band,
And Jacob's guitar playing skills were grand.
The man asked Jacob if he could play,
In his band called Summer's Day.

Jacob willingly agreed,
And did well in his career indeed,
His first ever concert was at Wembley,
And he was feeling rather trembly,
After the concert he had a bash,
And he now lives by the name of Slash.

Jack Sherratt (13)
Stafford Grammar School

A Life Like Cinderella

A lonely girl left alone,
In her cold, two bedroom, detached home,
Working in her stepdad's shop,
Scrubbing floors with her old mop.
A poor peasant girl, no use at all,
Working at her dad's fruit stall.

Prince C94 was his name,
They met at an unknown, online game.
He said, 'Come meet me at the Harvest Prom
Please be there, this is no con.'
She soon replied a giant, 'Yes!'
She would wear a beautiful, long, silk dress.

The bold bright lights like shining stars,
People racing like go-kart cars.
As they met under the disco ball,
Once taken out to the hollow hall.
Revealing him as one 'Charlie More',
Surprised so much, she was not sure.

The clock approached the dreaded hour,
She had to leave the joyful power.
Her stepdad travelling to the shop,
She had to run against the clock,
She reached the door and fled,
Poor Charlie looking all bereft.

His big rugby game soon crept along,
Spectators supporting, singing their song.
She decided to tell him about last night,
The dress, her Cinderella story height.
'I was the one last night, in the long silk dress?'
'Oh my,' he said, 'I have to say you were the best dressed.'

Emily Caplan (12)
Stafford Grammar School

True Friendship

My name is Haley,
And I have a best friend whose name is Jamie.
We met each other when we were about three,
When both our mums were having a cup of tea.
In high school we went together,
And in sixth form sat on seats of leather.

Jamie has hair that is curly and blonde,
But it went all straight when he fell in the pond,
I have hair that is long and brown,
But I always wear it up when I go into town.
Jamie is very tall,
And unfortunately I am very small.

Jamie's place is like a king and queen's palace,
But he has to share it with his sister named Alice.
I have a much smaller house,
I'm sure it's a house for a mouse.
Jamie's garden is also very big,
I've helped to plant flowers there so had to dig and dig.

Jamie tried to scare me in the forest one night,
I'd told him not to and of course I was right.
Because deep in the forest so dark,
He tripped over a piece of bark.
I didn't want to leave him,
But he'd hurt his foot and chin.

He went to A and E,
And had a doctor called Lee.
It turned out he only had a sprain,
But he was still in a great deal of pain.
He had also quite badly hurt his lip,
We're still friends, now this shows true friendship.

Helen Skilton (12)
Stafford Grammar School

Why Me?

Isolated, heart-pounding,
Dreading the day that lies ahead.
No way of preparing,
No way of knowing.
Why me?

I feel like a child, alone in the dark.
So many people are around me
Yet still I am overcome by loneliness,
At the centre of attention,
Yet still alone.
Why me?

I hurt them never
But I am a punchbag,
Absorbing impact after impact,
Struck viciously by words and kicks,
Why me?

I am trying to gain approval,
Doing all that I can,
But still I'm the target.
Why me?

I'm longing for the school bell,
Longing for help,
Longing to be included.
I wish they knew
They hurt me so much.
I can't let them know,
I hide it away
Deep, deep inside me.
Why? Why me?

Richard Jones (13)
Stafford Grammar School

The Cycle Of The Day

The day is breaking
The owls going to sleep
The sun is awakening
But the people, they weep.

The pollen dancing
In the summer's breeze
The people strolling
Through the big cities.

The world spinning unknowingly
In circles so big and round
The people they say boldly
'The weather's stormbound.'

The eagle watching its prey
Swooping from above
Planning its route like a runway
And putting it in his bed full of red.

The sun is beginning to tire
The owls are having their final dreams
But the young don't want to retire.

All the nocturnal things come out to play
The owls, the hamsters, the spiders
None of them enjoy the day
And neither do the robbers.

The owls wailing
The cameras watching the silent men
The wind howling
And waiting for this to start again!

Greg Moseley (14)
Stafford Grammar School

The Music

The curtain rises -
Suddenly
directed upon me
is the attention, undivided, undiluted
of hundreds

The hours spent
toiling
to prepare for these few minutes;
My one chance to make it all
worth it

To craft each note,
to make them sing
in a river, fluid;
to pick out each twig and stone and rock,
however heavy;
So my river flows,
perfect

I feel myself
shaking
under the weight
of a hundred hours, a hundred eyes
upon me

But this expectant sea of faces
is a blur;
They don't matter
as bow sets upon string;
Nothing matters.

Ann Lu (13)
Stafford Grammar School

Boo Boo

I was two when I first saw her.
She was beautiful.
She was everything I had hoped for.

Boo Boo,
That's what I called her.
That's how I remember her even today.

Boo Boo.
She went with me everywhere, even school.
I hid her in my bag, so no one ever knew.

Boo Boo.
She was with me on my first day to school,
She saw my first broken tooth, with me.
Was with me when I had my injections,
She was here,
And she was there, always,
By my side.

But then,
We were on the beach,
I left her to go for a little swim.
I didn't find her when I came back.
I lost Boo Boo.

I never knew where she went.
The thought never made me happy,
It just gave me realisation, and memories
Of the perfect hair and sweet blue eyes,
That had always made me smile.

Shreyasi Deshpande (13)
Stafford Grammar School

Crazy!

What's wrong with society,
When every time I look I see
Young girls dying to be on TV,
And not stopping till they reach their dreams?
Diet pills, surgery, supermodels in magazines,
Telling them who they should be.
It doesn't make sense to me.

What's wrong with society
Because everywhere I look I see,
Rich guys driving big SUVs,
While people are starving in the streets?

No one cares, no one likes to share,
I guess we're all too damn busy.
It doesn't make sense to me.

I guess things aren't how they used to be,
No more normal families,
Parents act like enemies,
Making kids feel like it's World War III.

No one's there, no one cares,
No one likes to share,
I guess life's unfair.

Is everybody going crazy?
Can anybody tell me what's going on?
Tell me what's going on
If you open your eyes,
You'll see that something is wrong!

Daniel Armstrong (14)
Stafford Grammar School

The Hooded Figure

I walked along a footpath one frosty winter's eve,
Treading through the snow coming up to my knees,
The forest I entered was unusually dark,
Unlike how it always was when I walked through that park.

To my surprise I heard a wolf howl,
I heard an owl hoot and a raging dog growl,
My heart was pounding, overcome by fear,
Barking and hissing invaded my ear.

I finally stopped running and sat on a tree,
When an elegant owl appeared next to me,
Its feathers were clouds, fluffy and white,
Then it left me in a graceful flight.

In the distance I saw a hooded figure,
He turned towards me and quietly sniggered,
Out from his robe, he drew a knife,
I turned around and ran for my life!

The man ran after me with the elegance of a brute,
I then cried in pain as I tripped over a tree root,
I looked back, red-faced, crippled by fright,
But there lay his dark cloak, the man was out of sight.

The way that man disappeared, to me is still unknown,
That was what I thought when my mum was on the phone,
She was calling a psychiatrist to come and talk to me,
But what I saw was definitely true,
No matter what anyone says to me.

Tom Appleford (11)
Stafford Grammar School

I Wish He Was Still Here Today

(A poem about my grandpa)

There's a photo very dear to me,
I look at it time and time again,
I'm with Grandpa at a party,
I can't be more than nine or ten,
We both are wearing silly hats
And grinning like Cheshire cats.

The pictures he skilfully painted
Are proudly displayed in our home,
He was a man of many talents
And in his spare time loved to roam,
Climbing mountains in the sun,
Living his life and having fun.

He wrote his life story in a book,
There's interest on every page,
If I had it here I'd let you look,
I'm sure that you would be amazed
To read of a life so full of toil
And of a man incredibly loyal.

Grandpa died in July this year
At the age of seventy-three;
The memories remain crystal-clear,
From the earliest, sitting on his knee.
He was special to me in every way,
I wish he was still here today.

Hannah Qureshi (14)
Stafford Grammar School

Death

Uncomfortable silences.
Sentences left unfinished.
Unnatural conversations echo through the grounds,
Filled with meaningless gestures,
All avoid the obvious subject.

Everyone files into the cold, stone pews
Like zombies, no word is said.

The coffin disappears into the ground
Like a lift descending.
The salty tears fall slowly and steadily.
A single red rose on the oak surface
Growing smaller and smaller
Each thorn a dagger in my heart.
In twos and threes the crowd disperses,
The bleakness is punctuated
By the crater-like wreaths
On surrounding gravestones.

A solitary figure revisits
His memories
At the grave where his loved one lies.

Death, a venture in to the unknown.
No way back.
Abandoned?
Bereft?
Is this the end?

Sean Phillips (13)
Stafford Grammar School

A Wonderful Time Of Year

The opening of the loft hatch door,
Sends the ladder crashing to the floor,
Millions of dust particles fill the air,
Dancing and floating without a care.
It's a wonderful time of year.

The light flickers on and shines around,
My beating heart begins to pound.
I can't believe it, it couldn't be true,
The carnage and destruction within my view!
It's a wonderful time of year.

A sinking feeling fills my shoes,
The heaviness gives me the blues.
Frantically I beckon to my mum,
'Where's the fire? I'm coming son!'
It's a wonderful time of year.

Shredded tinsel tossed about,
There's been a party, there's no doubt.
I'm nauseous and feeling sick,
I want to give these mice a kick!
It's a wonderful time of year.

The festive season's drawing near,
So why'd I want to shed a tear?
Oh no, surely it isn't to be,
My wonderful, perfect Christmas tree.
It's a wonderful time of year.

Joe Barnes (12)
Stafford Grammar School

The Lancaster

The Lancaster sits and swelters in the sun.
She is a gentle surveyor of destruction.
Gently her wings rock in the light breeze.
The giant wheels trying to break free from the taming chocks.

The siren sounds
And the hurried crew race towards the body of her.
As her four Merlin engines start their shift,
A splatter of machine gun-like fire from the exhaust.

A placid roar fills her hangers.
She advances her taxi, into position.
Abruptly her gentle roar,
Turns into a violent growl.

The soft air glides over the delicate wings,
The swan takes flight.

Her voice joins the choir of birds.
Her stomach filled with her deadly punch.

She rolls to her left
Accompanied by her baby sons,
Fighters protecting their mother,
Forming a chorus of their own.

Her roll levels out,
To a smooth flight.
Flying her flag
To her final destination.

Fraser Gillcrist Smith (14)
Stafford Grammar School

A Journey Through Africa

A tall white man was travelling steady
Through Africa, still unsure and not ready.
In his world it was either black or white,
To him like the differences of day and night.

Would he pick coffee or milk?
Definitely the milk for it looked like white silk.
Only leaving his home in the hours of daylight,
He only chose this, as it was brighter than night.

Entering the bar, wherever he sat he'd stick,
The fat or the thin he'd have to pick.
He sat next to the thin, who wasn't bothered in the slightest,
Our man thought the fat would've been tightest.

Next morning the man walked down the street,
Many poor people fell at his feet.
He ignored them all and carried on to the rich,
Left them to squirm, worms in a ditch.

One day the man felt queasy and ill,
He didn't know what to do, he had not one pill.
He headed to the doctor and was shocked to hear,
He had a fault with his heart, 'Oh dear, oh dear!'

The only option was to have the heart of an African man,
He said, 'Yeah sure, put it in as fast as you can!'
After the operation the man thought it through in his brain,
The way he would live, would never be the same.

Jordan Lane (13)
Stafford Grammar School

Big Fat Cat

I am a big fat cat,
I am not much but fur
But I can kill a rat
And have a lovely melodious purr.

I can be loveable, playful and bright,
Move my tail in the air and make it curled,
Sleepy by day and active by night,
And then I feel like the king of the world.

I climb up the highest trees
And if a bird sees me they flee,
But if they try to hide,
They will be in my tummy, all filled inside.

The feral cats pick on me for a fight,
I nail them with a scratch and a bite,
Now no one ever picks on me,
I am too strong for them you see.

I have my little clan of cats,
We hunt down all the mice and rats,
You may ask why we kill these poor creatures,
The reason is, they're dumb and stupid features.

But what I love most is my owner,
I impress them by being a show boater,
They think I'm so loveable and cute,
But they don't know the real me, I'm really a big brute.

Faris Raza (12)
Stafford Grammar School

Friends Forever

At Chester Hill High School,
There are children that are rich and cool.
Whereas some children are poor and kind,
Friends are people you cannot always find.

The poorest girl in school is Jade,
Who has got no friends that she has made.
With brown straight sticks on her head,
And her eyes look like they are made of lead.

But the richest girl in school is Vicki,
Who when it comes to friends, is very picky.
Vicki's ambition is anything to do with art,
Which is good because she is not very smart.

On the first day of their new school,
Vicki is seen as attractive and cool.
Jade is upset as she is seen as ugly and poor,
But the more she gets upset they say it even more!

When it comes to lunch time at the same time every day,
Jade doesn't want to eat and she doesn't want to play.
Guiltiness is starting to occur inside Vicki's head,
Jade is so upset she just wishes she was dead!

After two dreadful weeks, the end of school came,
Vicki approached Jade as if she did not know where to aim.
The words that she spoke were extremely shocking,
As Vicki asked Jade if she would be her friend and go shopping!

Lauren-Jayne Hill (12)
Stafford Grammar School

Audience

The wave of people with eyes that stare,
Their joy and enthusiasm fills the air.
At a place where patience and expectances meet,
They all dash around to find their seat.
Before the awaiting performance can greet.
A home in the audience's mind.

Once the opening performance begins,
The crowd hush down and there's silence within.
All eyes are turned to the figure on the stage.
Who is acting out happiness, anger and rage,
Flowing like water are the words that he speaks,
Flowing into the audience's minds.

By now all emotions are running on a high,
The tears and the laughter are starting to lie
On the faces of people sat down in the stalls,
Engulfed in the darkness till the curtain falls.
Each with a similar smile on their face,
And excitement in the audience's minds.

The tale that was told has now come to an end.
The message was woven and now it will send,
The people who come from near and from far
Back to the comforting homes in their cars,
Ladies and gentlemen and children alike,
Share the bond of the audience's mind.

Adam Handford (13)
Stafford Grammar School

My Brother

He waits to pounce on any error.
He is a winner even when he loses.
He is not afraid to be a terror
Doing all that he chooses.
Sometimes he's quiet, not making a sound.
Sometimes he's good, not messing around.

He's gone on many school trips
For science, geography and history.
He often forgets to hand in the slips.
Why he does it is still a mystery.
With his fishing rod he often goes out,
Always hoping he will catch a trout.

He loves his tennis, football and cricket
And he plays as much as he can.
He even watches Liverpool if he gets a ticket
From his good friend named Dan.
'Come on Liverpool!' he shouts out loud,
Along with thousands of others in the crowd.

He loves to holiday in the sun
And likes to feel so tanned.
He plays and swims and loves to run
For miles along the sand.
He brushes his hair to attract the girls.
He likes it straight and hates the curls.

Harry Bowers (13)
Stafford Grammar School

The Crystal Landscape

A blizzard cloaked the icy land,
Its divine force was a masterful hand,
It flowed and whispered through the tree,
Crystal snowflakes floated on its harsh breeze.
A polar bear trudged through the ice, looking slightly haggard,
Icicles hung from the icy cliff like deadly frozen daggers.

An almighty clash shook the ice,
Two duelling elks were locked in fight.
The clash of antlers was like war drums.
The vibrations caused a resonant hum.
Like water and fire their battle raged on.
It was now time for the setting of the sun.

Evening in the tundra, life had died down,
The wind had stopped moaning, settling to a frown,
The arctic hare had stopped its hop,
The moon had taken a sudden drop,
The sky had changed, it had turned dark,
An Arctic wolf was howling up to the stars.

Night in the tundra, wolves began their prowl,
One had spotted a stray rabbit signalled with a scowl.
The furry creature was frozen, the wolf was its blight,
The wolf sprang through the air into the twilight.
The wolf was bearing down on it, it tried to run.
It was the cycle of the tundra that had once more begun.

Joe Yates (13)
Stafford Grammar School

My Grandad

My grandad is the man,
Always helping around the house,
Doing whatever he can.
Yes, that's my grandad but he's really a mouse.
He has a bellowing voice,
And when we don't want to listen we have no choice.

You could say that he is old,
He's the proud owner of a butcher's shop.
He's always working at his shop, he'll never be told,
Nope, my grandad is always working, I don't think he'll ever stop!
He lives in the country like me
And likes his daily cup of tea.

On Sunday he stays at home and does whatever needs doing,
Whether it's having a bonfire or painting the shed.
He even does the washing!
After another hard day's work he's ready for bed.
In for nine and out by seven every day.
He's an early fellow.

He has worked very hard all of his life,
And for that I am very grateful.
To me the man is the best, the very tip of the knife.
He has been very careful.
Throughout the years saving every penny.
All of which has been for my family.

Edward Tyler (13)
Stafford Grammar School

My Grandad

He was a family man
We gave him love,
He always had a master plan,
He was a dove,
As tall as a tree,
He was always happy.

He was an eternal light,
He was charming,
We still dream of him at night,
He was witty and sparkling
He was well respected
And smelt splendid.

A light at the end of the tunnel.
Over the world towering,
If he was upset he wouldn't tell,
Mightily amusing.
As fit as a fiddle,
He always had to solve a riddle.

He was really cool,
He was very slim,
Never acted the fool,
He always said my hair needed a trim,
He used to eat nuts,
Then his eyes shut.

Matt Jones (13)
Stafford Grammar School

My Mum

She has an average life - for her it is,
Amongst the caring and looking after me.
Past the feelings she gets when she is cross,
She can be as busy as a big bee.
Out of bed, breakfast time then off to work,
Drops me off, hurries on while I smirk.

I know she is busy, doing a lot,
Filing papers and sorting out lunchtimes,
Marking dinners with pencil and dot,
Helping the children with their words and rhymes.
The end of the day comes, what a relief,
Shaking off exhaustion to keep belief.

But her day is not over, it's nearly though,
She gets home to get her kit for the gym.
And off we shoot, to gym, never too slow,
Trying to get thin, trying to get slim.
And then back home, knowing how well we did,
To get the pots out, also the lid.

Tea is chicken, pasta, or even stew,
Sometimes we go out as three,
(Mum, sister and I)
Has a bath, watches TV and drinks tea.
Relaxes and then it's time to go to bed,
Ready for another average day played.

Ross Hodgkins (14)
Stafford Grammar School

I Know Who You Really Are

Every day I come to school,
I have to talk with you.

Okay you want to know,
What's really happening to me?

I will tell you,
All you like to do is
Sit there talking about this and that,
But it's just not really cool.

You think you're cool but,
I know who you really are,
Inside your core.

So don't put on a false
Front to be everything
Because you're not.

You need to stop
And listen once.

Just because you are one
Of them doesn't mean you can't transmute.

Gyrate around and you'll find your true self,
Who really cares if you're cool?
It doesn't denote that you have
To be a *bully!*

Aaron Singh (13)
Stafford Grammar School

Gardening

The roses bloomed over her white skin,
Purple and red blossoming from dirty green.
Her nails had cracked from attempts at pruning
But hiding them just kept them growing.
She cried a hundred times over their anger,
Her white tears enough to feed their hunger;
Their compost the stale stain of wine
As their roots spread deeper than bone.

He lent her cuttings from his own garden,
Coaxing their fiery colours to brighten,
Illuminating her arms legs neck eyes
Until you couldn't distinguish skin from rose.
Eventually she returned the favours
Ploughing up his flesh with timid fingers,
But no flowers grew from corded muscle,
He was barren now; cold and bestial.

A blizzard of punches arrived one night,
Stinking of beer, fags and unrealised hate.
Like a suffocating pillow of snow
Her breath leached from her at each fist he threw,
Shredding the petals all over the floor;
The sweet aroma of blood coated the air.
Her body was cold as the soil froze stiff
But when he wept he wept for himself.

Elizabeth Egan (17)
Stafford Grammar School

Monty's Jackbauer

Black silhouette,
Sprinting down a never-ending track.

Uncared for and unloved.
Retired from racing,
But luckily rescued as so many aren't.

Escaped from certain death.

Alone he lived in a kennel,
Longing for company once more.
Seeing him all scruffy,
Thin and scarred,
We took him home,
Loved him, fed him
And groomed him.

Racing is now a distant memory
Now chasing rabbits,
In his sleep,
He dreams of happier things.

Now he's our lazy, healthy,
Happy dog.
Now a silhouette of shining black onyx.
Joey is our boy.

Ours forever.

Olivia Cheung (13)
Stafford Grammar School

Heartstrings

Beautiful, divine, sophisticated
Her curves are exquisite
Confidently posing in the light
Elegant, vivid
I hold her in my hands
Her neck, smooth
Enthralled, I strum.

Yash Gupta (13)
Stafford Grammar School

The Zoo

One day I went to the zoo with my friend,
Who ended up in a very sticky end.
The crocodile snapped and swallowed him whole,
He tried to escape, clawing the ground like a mole.
A lion broke in, all big and uppity,
It swallowed the croc! Oh what a calamity.
The next thing I knew, a gorilla was in there,
It swallowed the lion,
All claws, teeth and hair.
I watched in horror, the gorilla vanished from view,
Replaced by a python and that was when I knew
I had to save him!
From the teeth and the claws,
So I rolled up my sleeves and that was when I saw
The snake was swaying, it was going to blow.
It threw up the gorilla. That's right! I know!
The gorilla looked troubled and then from behind,
Appeared the lion, gassed out of its mind.
The lion returned, back to its place,
The snappety crocodile, an angry look on its face.
My friend then came out of the croc's open mouth,
Looking frozen solid, as if at the pole of the south.
I walked him home and he gave me a tip,
'Going to the zoo, is not a fun trip!

George Roland Goodwin (11)
Stafford Grammar School

Sunset On Lake Windermere

Dramatic sunlight bouncing and shining on the lake.
Multicolours in the sky forming silhouettes on the water.
The road was strewn with golden chestnuts fallen
fresh from the trees.
Autumn rays of sunlight searching for a gap between the trees.
The crispy, crunchy crackle was loud underneath my icy feet.
The freezing wind slapped my face and blew my hair askew.
Oh how I love an autumn day with nothing much to do!

Ambar Mumtaz Iqbal (11)
Stafford Grammar School

Sisters

My baby sister,
Still and silent, she lies in her cot.
My baby sister,
Her tiny face, her piercing cry.
My baby sister,
Soft silky skin, so smooth to the touch.
My baby sister,
Her cheeky little smile, shines in the sun.
My baby sister,
So small, so sweet.
My baby sister,
Tiny hands, tiny feet.
My baby sister,
Her funny, sweet ways.
My baby sister,
Peering out through the cot.
My baby sister,
I love her a lot.
My baby sister,
She laughs when we play.
My baby sister,
She fills my day . . .
With sunshine and laughter
In every possible way.

Ellie Miller (13)
Stafford Grammar School

The Animals Of Nature

The pure-coated swans,
Gracefully dance down the tiny, narrow pond.
The cat starts to stretch,
In the mid-afternoon,
This makes her body long.

Horses galloping throughout the day,
Jumping and rushing,
To find a barrel of hay.
As soon as they have found it and left
There will be no more.

The moose's antlers,
Stand sturdy and bold,
The baby chick's glowing beak,
And his fresh feathers painted gold.

The birds are hard workers as they construct their nest,
Spending hours so it will look its best.
They love to play and take a rest,
In the comfort of their freshly made nest.

Dancing in the sky,
The butterflies drift with the wind
The fireflies glow,
Creating a sun in the deadly night.

Emily Jackson (13)
Stafford Grammar School

The Magpie

A black and white blur of feathers,
Sits in her nest,
Whatever the weather.

Her wings spread out,
She jumps so high,
Oh my, oh my, she starts to fly.

Her beak, it holds a wonderful noise,
But when she lands,
It's all about poise.

The beautiful magpie swoops in flight.
And protects her eggs,
All through the night.

Collecting twigs for her nest,
It's a wonder she'll ever
Get some rest.

I saw her again yesterday,
As soon as my mum came,
She flew away.

She was in the garden, so was I.
I love her so much,
My little magpie.

Darcy Evans (10)
Stafford Grammar School

The Earl Of Kent

He whipped her with intent
As he was the Earl of Kent,
The deathly plan was foiled,
Which meant his pants were boiled.

The Earl ordered him around
By giving him a pound,
However the prisoner awoke,
To find all his fingers broke.

There was a man called Robin,
Who heard the prisoner sobbin',
Robin was a saint,
Who'd make the girls faint.

Robin shot his long arrow,
As high as Kilimanjaro,
The arrow came back down
And landed on the crown.

The Earl ran off to Dartford,
While Robin saved Hartford,
Robin Hood became king,
While the Earl didn't know a thing.

Matthew Thomas (12)
Stafford Grammar School

War

The silence was shattered by
The planes flying across the sky,
Coming to bomb down on Birmingham,
Going to the slaughter like a little lamb.

The Nazi swastika stained on planes,
Drawing near to the city's lanes.
People scared and worried at home;
Left in the darkness and all alone.

The war is a most horrible time,
For everyone knows of Hitler's crime:
To take all the people he does not care for;
And dispose of them is an appalling gore.

Out on the front line of defence,
Where there is a good moral sense.
The rattle of machine gun can be heard;
A gun the English have always preferred.

But when the war is at its end,
Some soldiers may have lost a friend.
Hopefully it'll never happen again;
So death will never be in vain.

Richard Cumberlidge (12)
Stafford Grammar School

Photo Album

Who's that?
That is your uncle Billy,
Who's that?
Your dad being silly.

Who's that?
That's your mum in her school play.
Who's that?
Polly, asleep at the end of the day.

Who's that?
The twins, Pop and Lolly,
Who's that?
Your gran and her brand new dolly.

Who's that?
It's you with ice cream all over your face,
Who's that?
Your sister on holiday with her suitcase.

Who's that?
Us all after Christmas dinner,
Who's that?
Me, proud to be a winner.

Ruth Knight (11)
Stafford Grammar School

Twin Towers

It was a lovely September day,
And you could see the towers from miles away,
They stood up straight so very high,
Like they almost reached the sky.

But this is now and that was then,
The New York skyline was never the same again,
The towers, they no longer remain,
And New York would never be the same.

Disaster struck as the planes hit,
And the towers crumbled bit by bit.
Was it an accident or not
Or was it just a terrorist plot?

So many lost their lives that day,
But will be remembered in every way,
The death, destruction and the terror,
Will be felt by the whole world forever.

We try and put this behind,
But somehow it is still stuck in our minds.
The 11th of September,
Is a day we will all remember.

Dan Nowell (13)
Stafford Grammar School

The River

In the river not far along,
The birds surrounding sing a song.
The little tadpoles swimming up and down,
Acting like baby clowns.

Along the river a fish swims,
He has shiny little fins.
The sun burning down on the river,
Shoots across the water ripples.

The thundering waterfalls are a washing machine,
Thrashing around, being cleaned.
As the river winds downstream,
The murky water turns to green.

As it races towards the coast.
The salty smell of seagulls is in the air.
Trickling past the seaweed's long floating hair,
Never stopping to show any care.

As the river comes to an end,
With one last spring around the bend.
The ocean's mouth is open wide,
Waiting to swallow it inside.

Emma Hamplett (11)
Stafford Grammar School

Why Bullies Bully

Alex was a cold-blooded bully,
He bullied every living thing.
And he was extremely lethal,
For on his finger he held a very big ring.

His main victim was a boy called Billy,
Small, skinny and scared was he,
As Alex came forward with fists at the ready
Billy felt as small as a pea.

Billy was brutally bashed by the bully,
Blood and bruises all over him,
Alex felt very happy,
As Billy's life was very dim.

His eyes were filled with sorrow,
And the bully's eyes were crammed with joy,
But after school they switched to fright,
As the dad beat his own boy.

This is why the bully bullies,
Because the dad hits his son,
He does it to let his anger out,
He never does it just for fun.

Daniel Foster (13)
Stafford Grammar School

Heaven

Out there somewhere
Angels fly around,
It may seem like a dream or a wish
But people do believe that angels really exist.
I believe, do you?

People who have gone,
And will never come back
Must get lonely up there.
Some miss their friends down here,
They are all alone!

Think about it,
Every time a person dies,
A new one is born,
Just a little happy thought to cheer you up
What do they get up to in Heaven? I wonder.

Most elderly people go to Heaven,
So if you've had an argument,
Make up with them because
When they have gone,
You'll miss them like never before!

Amy Everitt (11)
Stafford Grammar School

My Kinda Sport

There are different types of sport,
Like football, rugby and tennis on a court.
All of the sports use a ball,
I could stand in their shadows, which means they're tall.
Tennis players use their rackets,
On a football pitch they shout, 'Whack it!'
Swimming is done in a very large pool,
The water can be sometimes cool.
My dad's golf swing is quite mad.
But then again, my skiing is so bad!
In the boxing ring the fighters are brave,
Wow goalkeeper, a brilliant save!
At the hockey, the crashing of sticks,
If you're good enough you will get picked.
The snooker player goes for the black,
Horse riders will go on a hack.
All the cricketers wear their whites,
Not very often do they have fights.
Jensen Button takes the last bend,
Our F1 champion in the end.

Will Conn (12)
Stafford Grammar School

The Fall Of Troy

What am I doing here?
It's cramped and rather smelly.
Only the gods would know,
Why I'm stuck in the horse's belly.
Ten years this war's been on,
And I've lost the will to fight.
Oh well, it'll all be over
After this cold and bloody night.
'Stop fidgeting back there you fool,
You're going to get us caught!'
And once they realise they've been tricked,
They're sure to be distraught.
I've wet my sword with Trojan blood a thousand times before,
Just one more night of savageness, till the end of this damn war.
Night is upon us now,
It's time to draw your swords
'It's our time now men
Let's join the hall of Lords.'

Frederick Hutchinson (15)
Stafford Grammar School

My Spooky Thoughts

Counting sheep, counting sheep!
That's really not helping me to sleep.

Hour upon hour, I've laid in bed,
Trying to clear these thoughts from my head.

Howling winds and lashing rain,
Are thrashing at my window pane,

My eyes are closed but still I can see,
All these images that are terrifying me.

Of witches, ghouls and bats swooping low,
Of rats and snakes, spiders too.

Monster trees bend and creak,
In the dead of night it seems so bleak.

I pull up the covers right up to my chin,
But still I imagine they are climbing in.

The house is all quiet except for my clock,
For the millionth time it shouts, *'Tick-tock!'*

Sally Tyler (11)
Stafford Grammar School

Poor Old George

Poor old George, he's got in a mess,
He's got stuck in the trouser press.
Looking at his body, that's turned into a mat,
I think we all now feel quite flat.
Now he's got a permanent crease.
Poor old George is pressed in peace.
We'll miss him now his smile has gone.
No more him.
No more fun.
I miss having that bunny around.
I miss his smile but not his frown.
Now he's got a permanent crease,
Poor old George is pressed in peace.

Harry Handford (11)
Stafford Grammar School

Spring

Sitting beneath the blossom tree
Gazing at the gentle petals
As they floated down beside me
I listened to the birds sing their song
I smiled, raised my head to the clouds
And began to hum along.

I gazed upon the buzzing bees
Hovering around the neon flowers
They swayed and whirled and danced in the breeze
Drifting afar from the spring showers
Watching the water lilies bloom
Over this spring day, now I swooned.

What a beautiful spring morn
Looking at the river glisten
A beautiful spring day was born
To these blue birds I listened
What a beautiful, captivating spring day
Pure bliss and peace I would say.

Leah Coley-Fisher (14)
Stafford Grammar School

Christmas Day

Christmas morning, oh Christmas morning.
Waking up yawning from last night's late television light.
Creeping downstairs to see my gifts.
And when I see them, oh what a lift.

When I look outside and see the snow
It reminds me of my old white blanket.
But not forgetting on this day
Is also a time to remember Jesus and where He lay.

When I sit down to eat my dinner
It makes me feel like a Christmas winner.
When the day is drawing to an end
I practise my handwriting for the thank you letters I have to send.

Liam Buckley (12)
Stafford Grammar School

Unhappiness

The plates were smashed
Mum's car was crashed
The tears rolled down her face
A job was lost
The car had cost
Dad cried, 'What a waste!'

A brother's punch
Forgotten lunch
He hoped this day would end
Spoke to his crush
His heart was mush
Would it ever mend?

He wandered around
The vast playground
With not a friend in sight
The bully came
To play his game
Guess who won the fight.

Philippa Davis (14)
Stafford Grammar School

Urban Decay

Birds chirping their lullaby,
Cars and people pass me by,
Sitting here all alone,
Nowhere to call home.

Money dropping by my side,
Cities and nature begin to collide,
Litter scattered down the street,
People stepping on my feet.

Look to my right,
What a beautiful sight,
Lush green grass and beautiful flowers,
Everything damp from the mid-morning showers.

Hannah Anderson (14)
Stafford Grammar School

An Autumn Day

On autumn days I take a walk in the countryside. Walking along the country path I hear the twigs crunching under my feet. I think of them as Christmas crackers, making loud and unexpected noises. It's a cold time of year and I hug my coat round me to keep the cold at bay. Walking further, I find a large old oak tree, gnarled with age. Squirrels race up and down it, a blur as they collect provisions for the fast coming winter months. They move about noisily, chittering and chattering and taking a quick bite out of an acorn as a snack. Their claws make scratching sounds on the leaves. Moving on, it goes quiet, so I start to kick leaves as I like the crunching noise. Doing so, I feel something on my shoe. I think maybe it will be holly, but bending down see a small brown ball. It is a tennis ball, with skewers sticking out at all angles. Putting the hedgehog down I bury it carefully in dried leaves, putting it at the side of the path so it won't be unfortunate again. It is starting to become a very nice day, as the sun is coming out. Up ahead I see a robin perched on a branch, its shrill training whistle voice being heard above all the birds' voices beside itself. Then, I come to it. The wood, I hear tiny creatures scratching about like nails on a wooden door. This is my entrance to further autumnal adventures.

Lizzie Hyde (11)
Stafford Grammar School

To You, From Me

A gift, my dear,
For you, from me,
To lose those tears,
And fill you with glee.
In times you're sad,
Or when you cry,
Of if you're mad,
To pass the time by.
A book, my dear,
For you to see,
Full of memories.
Of you and me.
So next time that you're feeling down,
Just have a look and lose that frown.

William Moorcroft (15)
Stafford Grammar School

Hole

Not the hole you dig at the beach
And push your friends into.

Not the satiny night sky,
You see through a Red Indian's shelter.

But the hole that digs down far deeper than others.
The wound.
The hole.

Waiting.
'Time heals,' they say, but how long will that take?

Hollow as oak you laugh,
Not a flicker of pain you show.

Yet deep inside you're softly weeping.
A pain like flint can crop up while you're sleeping

But love keeps you going and friendship and life,
Living each day, with a hole deep inside.

Becky Louise Kohler (14)
Stafford Grammar School

I'm On The Bus To School

Looking around at all my friends sleeping,
Uh oh, Sam's just about to drool!
His legs start twitching,
He must be having that dream again.
The one where he's chasing rabbits,
Sam likes to pretend,
That he's a farmer chasing them away from the cabbages.

We arrive at school,
It is very wet as it is raining.
Trust the bus driver, he stops by a puddle as big as a pool!
Sam's jumping.
He lands smack bang in the middle.
Soaking already, he goes off to play football with Harry.
Josh joins in with his boots from Lidl.

James Lewis (14)
Stafford Grammar School

The Winter Forest

I walk along the forest path
And watch the morning mist creep
Along the rugged and withered ground
That supports the mighty pillars,
That supports the alpine trees.

I walk along the forest path
And sit down by the lake.
The cold air chills my every bone
As I watch the water move freely,
As I watch the water dance with the wind.

Snow covers the ground I walk on,
It covers the regal trees.
The forest is covered in winter's blanket.
The wildlife scurry back to their dwellings
As the moon draws the curtain on the day.

Danylo Dubil (13)
Stafford Grammar School

The Tap

Drip, drop goes the tap,
My bathroom is dark and black,
Shower's dead with dust,
Old bath is starting to rust.

The splashing of water starts to get loud,
Like a puddle of water straight from a cloud.

The bathroom's always empty in this house,
One thing goes in there but it's only a mouse.

A year has passed, finally at last,
Our bathroom gets re-done,
Shower is a shining sun and bath smells
As lovely as a plum.

Taps don't drip or drop anymore
And the mouse has been kicked out the door.

Jacob Ferguson (14)
Stafford Grammar School

I Saw A Ghost

I saw a ghost deep into the night,
It touched me on the back and gave me a fright,
I said to the ghost, 'Go away, go away!'
He said, 'No,' as he wanted to stay.

The ghoul floated round me in the air,
Crept up behind me, then pulled my hair,
I called for Dad, but he was asleep,
The ghost tried to pull me, so I made a leap.

I ran out of my room, I was very fast,
The ghost followed me, but I knew he was last,
I sprinted downstairs into the hallway,
But he still followed me and wanted to stay.

I opened a drawer and pulled out a knife,
The ghost stared at me and ran for his life.
I closed all the windows and pulled down the blinds,
Then I went up to bed, to clear my mind.

Harry Redler (11)
Stafford Grammar School

The Great White Shark

I stood upon the boat
Anticipating
The signs of the predator
That I was about to see.

Without warning a dorsal fin
Appeared
Out of the deep blue darkness
Like a sail on the horizon.

Fearful I watched it
Thrashing about
A splash, a grin,
A snow-capped mountain range within.

Two shiny buttons watched me
Suspiciously
Swimming away into the inky well
Disappearing, the magician of the sea.

Alexander Langford (13)
Stafford Grammar School

The Ports On The Sea

There are ports on the sea,
For you and me.
There are ports on the sea for one and all
But mine's the best of all.

Full of lilac, full of roses,
Full of pretty, thornless roses.
Lots of lavender, lots of sweet pea.
It's the best and belongs to me.

Wonderful smells and wonderful sights
And no one ever fights.
Exotic smells and beautiful sights
And oh so many pretty lights.

Though its call is oh so strong,
To only one it may truly belong,
I'm so lucky, yes it's me,
That one time owner is me.

Sarah Taylor-Knight (12)
Stafford Grammar School

The Old Oak Tree

The old oak stands so tall
It towers as high as a giant
It looks down on all other trees
As if it were the king
The old oak tree is strong and bold
It would be a crime if its timber were sold

The tree stands firm
It won't even budge
The roots are the anchors
From the supreme Mary Rose

As the tree fights the gusts of wind
You know it is ancient
The tree has seen past generations grow old
And new generations being made
The oak tree has a lot of knowledge
Hidden inside its colossal trunk.

William Thomas (13)
Stafford Grammar School

One Night . . .

One night me and my gran went for a walk.
We sat on a park bench and began to talk.

'Ohh,' Gran said, 'I've just seen 3 witches go by,
knock on the door and go inside.'
'Oh Gran,' I said but she ignored me.
'Beware this night because this is the night that all goes wrong.'

She does this every year, she always forgets.
'There are 3 wolves in a pack, putting sweeties in their sack.'

'Run for the hills,' she shouted, 'Witches, wizards, werewolves, goblins,
gremlins, zombies and monsters!'

'Grandma!' I screamed.
'Yes Jimmy?' she said.
'All these things that you have seen,
Don't you realise it's Hallowe'en!'

George Edward Bunn (11)
Stafford Grammar School

Fire

Seen by man as death and destruction,
Truly he is the first part of reclamation and the end
which is purging,
To feel the warmth against your skin is unforgettable.

He needs to reclaim what is rightfully his before he shall be contained,
He must have it or to deny him what he wants
Will mean anger and he will consume everything.
To die by his hands shall purge you of all sins and allow further reclamation.

Purging is what he does,
Purging it to the ground sanctifies its fate
And brings it back to the Earth.
Purging is what he finds is right

Fire is not death and destruction,
It is purging and reclamation.

Morgan Williams (13)
The Polesworth School

The Girl From Stanley Head

Seasons come,
And seasons go,
Summers show
And raindrops flow,
But for the girl
On Stanley Head
A black cloud,
Is always over her head.

As she wanders into school,
People point and sneer,
Only if they knew, she thinks
And she dreads the home time bell ringing.

At last the bell rings
And she wanders home,
She wonders if for one more night,
She could be home alone.
She opens the door
And looks around,
Nobody's home, she thinks aloud.
She climbs on her bed,
So I guess she doesn't see,
The shadow in the corner,
Waiting for her to sleep.

The very next day,
The bullies wait,
She doesn't show
Her fake-smile face.

After school,
On a polished rock,
The fake-smile face,
What a shock.
'Here lies Elizabeth'
The polished rock says,
Do they realise
She won't wake?

Paige Evans (13)
The Polesworth School

These Are The Walls I Cannot Break

These are the walls I cannot break,
They will not tremble, quiver or shake,
And no matter how hard I try,
They box me in, lie after lie.

I can't reach out, there is no door,
False friendship kills me more and more,
'Hi' they say and walk away,
'Whatever' they never meant it anyway.

'How are you?' Like I'm some sort of queen,
With glistening jewels and crowns that gleam,
But I am no different to anyone else,
I have no problems with my health.

So why treat me like I'm the plague?
With a grinning smile, but eyes so vague,
They think they forge it oh so well,
But still they cannot hide the smell, of . . .

She thinks she's cool, she thinks she's great,
But still she does not see her fate,
She fails to ever realise,
That we see darkness in her eyes,

A teacher's pet, a nerdy wail,
Whoosh! She just blew off the scale,
She'll never be among the cool,
Chewing gum and skipping school.

She must think we are all her friends.
Screeching, 'Hi!' round every bend,
Yet we still do it for the sake,
Of knowing her perception, is just a mistake.

We know inside that little box,
She's really just the same as us,
But we won't let the truth prevail,
And venture through that stinging hail, that . . .

Eventually the truth will out,
I know this without any doubt,
My swollen soul, no different to yours,
With longing time it will soar.

Above the treetops, against the rain,
I'll say goodbye to my pain,
With my sibling by my side,
Maybe now they will subside,
Goodbye to that longing drone, this time . . . I am not alone.

Mabel Dandy (13)
The Polesworth School

Love

It's like a ball of happiness,
Running through your veins,
It leaves your emotions in a mess,
And causes a lot of pain.

You think it's gonna last,
But it's all just another game,
Can't put it in the past,
You keep hearing their name.

You don't know what to do,
Can't even think straight,
Just be you,
All you can do is wait.

A horrible night,
A horrible dream,
Wake up now,
It's easier than it seems.

Not long now,
Just moments to go,
Calm down love,
It's just a simple yes or no.

Claire Russell (13)
The Polesworth School

I Said I Was Sorry!

There she was, just staring at me
In the room of doom
There he was, just talking at me
In the room of gloom
I didn't mean to
It wasn't my fault
I said I was sorry
She ran in front of the car
I swerved
She screamed
There she was, just staring at me
In the room of doom
There he was, just talking at me
In the room of gloom
There she was just lying there
As a stone-cold corpse
There she was, just lying there
In her room of . . . *Death!*

Chloe Price (13)
The Polesworth School

The Fire Of The Bullies

I feel like fire, burning inside,
As these miserable bullies hit me with lies.
I scream and shout, but there's nowhere to go,
As I lie there still, unconscious in the snow.
The wind whips round me as I curl up tight,
Will those bullies pick another fight?
I dare to move, in case they come back,
Scared in case of getting another smack!
I hear a slight whisper, gently in my ear,
Telling me closely, the end is not here.
It tells me to stand up, look all around,
Look at the mountains, the trees, the ground.
The whisper, the whisper, tells me to tell,
All of those bullies, they'll end up in Hell.

Sam Butler (14)
The Polesworth School

Love

Love . . .
One minute you feel you're on top of the world,
The next your world comes crashing down.
Love's full of lies and regret,
Full of complication and jealousy.
It's like a deep hole.
It's easy to fall into.
But while you're in it
All the lies and regret
The complication and the jealousy fly away . . .
Then the happiness and the languid feelings take over.
Love's a never-ending cycle of emotions,
You never know when it's going to catch up with you next.

Faye Bassford (13)
The Polesworth School

Everything . . .

You are the earth under my house,
You are the air around my head,
You are the sounds from a mouse,
You are the words I have said,

You are the sparkle in a crystal,
You are the shine on amethyst,
You are the bullet in a pistol,
You are the strength in a fist.

You are the air I breathe,
And the things I see,
You are the thoughts I receive,
And you are everything to me!

Megan Chapman (13)
The Polesworth School

That Girl

I love that girl
With her long brown hair
When she does that twirl
Right over there.

She looked at me with her cute brown eyes
I stared in shock
While I was up the tree enjoying her lies
She was wearing a torn frock.

She came over
When her head went smack
Against the bathroom floor
And I found out she was on crack.

Tom Harris (13)
The Polesworth School

Homelessness

Toss a coin, did you win?
Would you take the chance, eat off a plate or bin?
Would you sleep on the floor,
Or would you rather sleep on more?
A bed, a mattress, that cosy quilt,
Should you feel sorrow, anger or guilt?
It was not a choice they chose to take,
Maybe it was chance or a mistake.
No one dreams of that cold stone floor,
They dream like you, they want more.
How dare we accuse, abuse, that makes us the bad cookie,
They just tossed a coin and got unlucky.

Sam Lewis (13)
The Polesworth School

I Miss You

I miss you, a piece of art
It's like a lock, next to my heart
Infinity, to find the key
And this painful misery, I miss you
A picture hanging on the wall
Of me and you at the ball
I shed a tear and give a smile
Now I'm waiting down the aisle
Wish me luck on my big day
I'll think of you all the way
So give me strength and show me faith
I cannot wait till we meet again . . . someday.

Cerys Roberts (13)
The Polesworth School

High Then Low

I'm in a dark place,
I want my own space,
I'm sick of this pain,
Just looking for that gain,
I sit alone in my room,
In the dark, black gloom,
I feel like I'm being killed,
Thought that stuff would make me thrilled,
Forget all this stuff,
I'm going for another putt.

Jonathan Hill (14)
The Polesworth School

Young Writers Information

We hope you have enjoyed reading this book - and that you will continue to enjoy it in the coming years.

If you like reading and writing poetry drop us a line, or give us a call, and we'll send you a free information pack.

Alternatively if you would like to order further copies of this book or any of our other titles, then please give us a call or log onto our website at www.youngwriters.co.uk

Young Writers Information
Remus House
Coltsfoot Drive
Peterborough
PE2 9JX
(01733) 890066